AF701688

GUIDANCE MONOGRAPH SERIES

SHELLEY C. STONE

BRUCE SHERTZER

Editors

GUIDANCE MONOGRAPH SERIES

The general purpose of Houghton Mifflin's Guidance Monograph Series is to provide high quality coverage of topics which are of abiding importance in contemporary counseling and guidance practice. In a rapidly expanding field of endeavor, change and innovation are inevitably present. A trend accompanying such growth is greater and greater specialization. Specialization results in an increased demand for materials which reflect current modifications in guidance practice while simultaneously treating the field in greater depth and detail than commonly found in textbooks and brief journal articles.

The list of eminent contributors to this series assures the reader expert treatment of the areas covered. The monographs are designed for consumers with varying familiarity to the counseling and guidance field. The editors believe that the series will be useful to experienced practitioners as well as beginning students. While these groups may use the monographs with somewhat different goals in mind, both will benefit from the treatment given to content areas.

The content areas treated have been selected because of specific criteria. Among them are timeliness, practicality, and persistency of the issues involved. Above all, the editors have attempted to select topics which are of major substantive concern to counseling and guidance personnel.

Shelley C. Stone

Bruce Shertzer

SOCIAL CHANGE COUNSELING: A RADICAL APPROACH

MARILYN A. HUTCHINSON
HOLLY A. STADLER
PURDUE UNIVERSITY

HOUGHTON MIFFLIN COMPANY · BOSTON
ATLANTA · DALLAS · GENEVA, ILL. · HOPEWELL, N.J. · PALO ALTO

ISBN: 0–395–200407

Library of Congress Catalog Card
Number: 74–11965

Copyright © 1975 by Houghton Mifflin Company. *All rights reserved. No part of this work may be reproduced or transmitted in any form or by any means, electronic or mechanical, including photocopying and recording, or by any information storage or retrieval system, without permission in writing from the publisher. Printed in the U.S.A.*

CONTENTS

EDITORS' INTRODUCTION

Slightly more than a decade ago Edward J. Shoben, Jr. advanced the proposition that the purpose of counseling should be that of social reconstruction. Underlying his thesis was the assertion that counselors unwittingly smuggle middle class values and function to perpetuate — for a good or ill — society's institutions. Since Shoben's article appeared, many have concluded that the counselor ought to function as a change agent. This view of how counselors should function has occurred concurrently at a time of tremendous social upheaval and unrest in American society. This unrest has often focused on the need for institutional change and critical questioning of society's ways of responding to individuals who differ from the mythical, socially defined "normal" person.

Ms. Stadler and Ms. Hutchinson present a treatment of what they term "social change counseling." In this approach counselors function as declared change agents. Their efforts are directed toward facilitating the individual's well-being by means other than adjustment to existing situations. Rather, social change counseling requires extensive attention be given to the function that the environment, social institutions, political factors, etc. play in the creation and perpetuation of human concerns, unhappiness and problems. In this approach the alternative to confront and alter that which impinges on the counselor's clientele is viewed as viable and to be encouraged.

The content of this monograph ranges widely. It will be viewed by some as disturbing but by many as provocative and stimulating. Those reading it carefully with an open mind will be forced to examine their own philosophy and work as counselors, perhaps to the benefit of their clients and undoubtedly to the benefit of their own growth.

Shelley C. Stone
Bruce Shertzer

AUTHORS' INTRODUCTION

Social Change Counseling is a contemporary approach to working with people which makes the basic assumption that many of the difficulties which people encounter are not personal problems, something inside their heads, or even products of a particular family interaction; instead they result from the influences and effects of socialization and social institutions of our western culture. This approach borrows many of its tenets from contemporary writers, including the Radical Therapy approaches. A brief outline of the progression of psychological thought may be of assistance to put this and other theories in perspective.

Sigmund Freud, as the creator of psychoanalysis during the Victorian age, encapsulated many of the moral and sexual mores of his time. His premises primarily concerned the control of the pleasure wishes of individuals. This was very much the prevailing consensus in Victorian thought. To popular conceptions he added constructs concerning the unconscious, the natural inferiority of women, and the notion that anyone who questions what authorities (or therapists) propose as correct has a mental problem. This can only be changed, Freud declared, through extensive psychoanalysis which involves bringing one into touch with earlier developmental stages by reliving traumas and transferring unresolved feelings onto one's therapist.

Behaviorism gained popularity during the mid 1900's with its emphasis on learned problems. It was viewed by many as mechanistic during the 1950's and psychoanalysis was seen as more humane. However, both took a step back as a wave of humanism developed, viewing the therapeutic process as an interaction between two real people who could deal only with the present. Carl Rogers, the major proponent of client-centered therapy, felt that being in a relationship which was genuine would allow the client to grow. Eventually, by an unspecified process, the client was to transfer growth into the world at large, in which they had previously been unhappy.

None of these or other approaches seriously took into account the role of the environment and its possibility for change. Behaviorism accepts that the environment does exist and acknowledges its effects. It focuses on teaching the client skills or behaviors which will allow him or her to adapt more successfully to the environment.

During the early 1960's a small group of "anti-psychiatrists" began to write and advance new notions as to what might be the genesis of "personal" problems. The most well-known of these writers included R. D. Laing, Thomas Szasz, and Eric Goffman. Although they had specific differences they essentially agreed on four common assumptions: 1) that mental illness is a myth that society uses to avoid and cover-up the real problems; 2) that problems which a person presents can only be understood by exploring the social context and circumstances of that particular individual; 3) that psychiatric problems are not a product of individual deficiencies or deficits, but rather are a function of the world in which people live, and; 4) that psychiatry and psychology have played an oppressive role by adding to the social control of those who deviate.

Simultaneous with this development was a rise in encounter, awareness, Gestalt, and "touchy-feely" psychology and counseling. As before, these approaches failed to deal with the effect the world has had upon the individual. They attempted to help the bored and alienated in our culture find some relief. They did not question the culture which causes people to feel alienated, frightened and out of touch with themselves and others. They did not recognize the futility of their goal for everyone eventually to feel good as a result of encounter or therapeutic experiences.

During the late 1960's two independent groups emerged. In North Dakota the Radical Therapist Collective formed, initially starting community rap centers which tried to help others see the political realities of their situations. Eventually the collective began to organize and published *The Radical Therapist,* a newspaper and book of the same title. As their political awareness grew, they decided that being radical and being a therapist were mutually exclusive. As a therapist, one could only reinforce the status quo and could only oppress others in the hierarchical role of therapy. Self-help organizations were the only way in which they could reconcile their political beliefs with the psychological domain. In conjunction with this change, the newspaper was renamed *Rough Times.* A book which is a collection from the second year of publication has the same title. With *Rough Times* the emphasis moved from the therapeutic relationship in either individual or group counseling to a focus on aiding liberation groups: gay liberation, women's liberation, prisoners' rights groups, the Insane Liberation Front, and the liberation of black and all third world peoples. Their aim is to aid the liberation of all oppressed people here and abroad, through whatever reorganization of our society is required. The original Radical Therapy Collective included David Bryan, Linda Bryan, Michael Gallan, Michael Glenn, and Sara Glenn.

The second group is the outgrowth of a Free University course in Radical Psychiatry taught by Claude Steiner in Berkeley in 1969. In connection with Hogie Wycoff, a feminist activist of Berkeley, a RAP (Radical Approach to Psychiatry) Center was also established. Wycoff and Steiner worked to remove the hierarchies of the therapeutic relationship within their own work and continued teaching in the Free University at Berkeley. The approach used was an extension of transactional analysis. Additional components such as the life scripts of women, and the stroke economy as a means of maintaining social control and regulating conformity were examined.

During the 1970's these and other groups have struggled to find a psychology which reflects a Marxian view of society's organization, the conflict theory of Chairman Mao Tse Tung, and values other than those of the American middle class. Those efforts have not been fruitful.

It is at this juncture that Social Change Counseling originates. As practicing counselors in the community and college environments, the authors are painfully aware of the role that the institutions we represent play in creating problems for our clients. We recognize that sex, class, and racial stereotyping limit and confine those who might otherwise grow. It is also with distress that we examine how we, despite our desire not to do so, have also oppressed those who have sought help from us. We have taught shy men how to be more acceptable dating partners, thus perpetuating a system which is restrictive to both sexes. We have encouraged parents to take more control of their children, reinforcing the notions that children are the property of their parents and that elders always know best. We have maintained distance from our clients, not sharing with them our own anxiety, frustrations and disappointments because the role of therapist is not defined in such a manner. We have talked about cases, not people, have identified our analysis of the "problem," and did not share our analysis with our clients because it did not seem to be proper therapeutically. Throughout the entire training and counseling process we have pretended to know what we were doing. In times of doubt we have maintained the hierarchy so that we were in the power position, and have taught clients to adjust to a world which needs changing.

Consequently the writing of this monograph serves two functions. First, it will share with you our perceptions of how the world might be viewed, a view which is not included in the analytic, behavioral, or humanistic theories of counseling and therapy. Perhaps as such, it will give some insights or views which you had not previously considered.

Secondly, it is an attempt by us to formulate more clearly how we perceive the counseling relationship, its potential, its hazards, its power and its weaknesses. In this regard this work is not definitive, for we find our awareness of political and social events growing as we read, talk, and try to apply our approach to new situations. As practicing counselors we have not been able to use only the theories which we were taught in graduate school for they fail to account for effects which we know operate in the lives of our clients. Simultaneously we have not been able to align ourselves with the radical therapists who see all problems as the result of social alienation and oppression. They call for the end of the therapeutic relationship and a dedication of liberation and freedom struggles by all who are concerned with the oppression. We think counseling need not oppress others. We can conceive of our skills as not bound by a role. Social Change Counseling is our attempt to conceptualize our work as counselors without compromising what we see as the reality of everyday lives.

M. A. Hutchinson
H. A. Stadler

ACKNOWLEDGEMENTS

We extend our thanks to Trudy Berkovitz, Janine Bernard, Christine Fischetti, Bruce Shertzer, Joel Silver, and Shelley Stone for their support, ideas and assistance in editing.

1

Theoretical Perspectives

The basic premise of a Social Change Counseling approach is that adjustment is not the only alternative which needs to be considered in a counseling situation. Making available alternatives other than adjustment to any situation which is intolerable or unjust is the mandate of this approach and therein it diverges from other types of therapy. Counseling (or therapy, or any psychological intervention) does not operate in a vacuum, insulated from society and the political structure. Each individual and each group are part of a greater whole, therefore, therapeutic interventions with a smaller part have implications for the greater part.

Certainly it is philosophically and professionally less threatening to scrutinize only the counselor-client relationship and its outcomes. This leaves unexamined the implications which the relationship and its outcomes may have for the groups of which counselor and client are members or for society as a whole. Social Change Counseling asserts that counselors must be aware of the social and political ramifications of their work. To date, counseling has functioned to preserve the status quo and has protected society's institutions. The Social Change approach departs from more traditional theories which contend that problems are rooted within the individual while society and its institutions remain blameless. Further discussion of the differences between these and the authors' approaches will be presented in later pages.

This chapter will draw from varied sources in an attempt to provide the background in a sociological, psychological and anthropological framework. The authors cited are certainly not all who have written about the political and sociological implications of counseling. They do, however, represent the range and development of thought over the last several decades. Each author will be considered singly in an effort to maintain the individuality of his/her contribution.

Thomas Merton

A contemporary sociologist at the Bureau of Applied Social Research at Columbia University and a frequently-published author in the realm of social structures and theories, Thomas Merton, in *Social Theory and Social Structure,* introduces two concepts which speak to a societal approach to counseling. These are his theories on *manifest and latent functions,* and the nature of social structure and *anomie.* Beginning with *manifest and latent functions,* Merton (1957, p. 51) describes the former as "objective consequences contributing to the adjustment or adaptation of the system which are intended or recognized by participants in those systems," while the latter functions are "neither intended nor recognized." The influence of such ideas on those who follow an activist approach to counseling and therapy has stimulated a questioning of the institutions and social structures encompassed by the helping professions. Asked are questions such as: what are the manifest functions of mental hospitals? of homes for juvenile offenders? of counseling relationships? What can be identified as the objective consequences of the establishment of these kinds of structures — the alleviation of mental illness? decline in the incidence of juvenile delinquency? movement toward effective independent functioning? Equally, if not more, important are questions pertaining to the latent functions of these structures, the unintended or unrecognized consequences. Is it possible that mental hospitals do more to subjugate and quiet society's outcasts than to treat mental illness? or that homes for juvenile offenders foster increased alienation rather than reentry into society? Could it be that counseling relationships reinforce adjustment to unresponsive social institutions without considering alternatives?

The answers to the questions concerning the latent functions of these structures may seem paradoxical, as Merton suggests, because they differ from the popular notions about the consequences of these structures. These seemingly paradoxical consequences are due to the difference between the manifest and latent functions of the structures.

Using the theory of functional analysis, Merton writes that one of the purposes in distinguishing between these two functions is to aid in the interpretation of the many social practices which do not appear to be achieving their stated goals. Despite the deficiencies of these practices, they may persist because of the latent functions they serve. Following this trend of thought societal counselors look at the antiquated and degrading mental hospitals as repositories for those unlucky individuals adjudged to be intolerably different by fellow members of society. They seem to serve no rehabilitative or mental health-enhancing function. Similarly many individuals have written of the possible purposes of the counseling relationship. The goals of this relationship are rarely stated in a measurable or testable manner, but research is indicating that the effectiveness of counseling and therapy is questionable (Eysenck, 1965). If the manifest functions of counseling-therapy are not being served, then, according to Merton, the focus should be directed to the latent functions. It is not implausible to suggest that one such function of the counseling relationship is to preserve the status quo, to suppress deviation from institutional norms (e.g. school, hospital, etc.).

An additional point which Merton brings up is an important one to mention at this time. He sets forth this basic theorem: "Any attempt to eliminate an existing social structure without providing adequate alternative structures for fulfilling the functions previously fulfilled by the abolished organization is doomed to failure [Merton, 1957, p. 81]." Merton goes on to say that unless alternative structures are formed to satisfy these needs or unless change occurs which will eliminate these needs, the abolished organization, in some form, will regain its lost position. Those of us who would aspire to replace some existing structures should take heed of this warning. We must functionally analyze these structures and then either provide for these needs in other ways or change the needs.

The second topic discussed by Merton, *anomie,* is also important to those concerned with an activist approach to counseling. Used by Durkheim and others, anomie has come to mean a condition of relative normlessness within a social order. This situation may be eventuated by social instability arising out of the dissociation of culturally prescribed aspirations and the socially ascribed avenues for realizing these aspirations (Merton, 1957). Many individuals find that the rewards for conforming to institutionalized norms are not sufficient to warrant the sacrifices of conformity. In the United States one encounters the situation in which there exists a clear emphasis on success goals with no concomitant emphasis on the institutional means of reaching these goals. The family, schools, and work all encourage striving for the success goals of our society, though many of these aspirations remain unfulfilled. For those interested in social change and its relation to counseling and therapy, the ways in which various individuals and groups respond to the pressure of such a social order are of great significance. Merton describes five types of individual adaptations: conformity (the acceptance of both cultural goals and institutionalized means of achieving these goals); innovation (acceptance of goals, rejection of means); ritualism (rejection of goals, acceptance of means); retreatism (rejection of goals and means); and rebellion (rejection of prevailing values and substitution of new values).

Though all five types are important, the last four represent aberrant forms of behavior. Innovation as a form of adaptation is founded on the premise that there exist in the society individuals who are imperfectly socialized so as to cast off the institutionalized means but still strive for the cultural goals. This frame of reference enhances risk taking as a method of achieving aspirations with much emphasis on luck and the Horatio Alger ethic. Innovative adaptation is a frequent tact taken by lower class individuals in coping with the pressures of the social order and is often manifested by criminal or delinquent behavior.

The third type of adaptation, ritualism, is marked by the frustration of trying to compete for cultural goals, resulting in the establishment of lowered and more easily satisfied aspirations. Persons of the lower middle class are generally found within this category, characterized by close adherence to cultural norms.

Since retreatism involves rejection of both goals and means, it is the least practiced form of adaptation. Society's displaced — the derelict, the addict, the psychotic and the bum— have continued to fail in achieving cultural goals by legitimate means and cannot sanction the use of illegitimate means. They have resolved the conflict by forsaking both goals and means.

The fifth and final type of adaptation which Merton describes is rebellion. Individuals within this category feel that the goals to which they aspire are legitimate ones but are unable to attain them because of obstructions created by the institutionalized system. These obstructions lead them outside of the present social structure, not in retreat, but to seek alternatives and to change the structure.

The constructs presented by Merton can offer the counselor or therapist striving for social change a conceptual framework within which to locate many types of socially or politically aberrant behavior. Perhaps if the identification of the style used by a particular individual is explained and made known to him/her, the choice of alternatives will be expanded. It is the aim of a Social Change Counseling theory to put forth such a framework as an alternative or supplement to more traditional therapeutic approaches (e.g. Rogerian, Freudian, Gestalt, Behavioral).

R. D. Laing

Laing's work has had a profound influence on the entire field of psychotherapy, not only on those concerned with social change. An especially significant contribution has been his theory of schizophrenia as a natural process in dealing with the alienation of everyday life. Though relatively few agree with this point, it has indeed provoked much thought and discussion. He developed this idea and other relevant concepts in his book *The Politics of Experience.* He expands upon Thomas Scheff's (1964) notion of the labeling of persons as schizophrenic as a social fact and political event. As Laing (1967, p. 121) asserts: "The behavior of the diagnosed patient is part of a much larger network of disturbed behavior. The contradictions and confusions internalized by the individuals must be looked at in their larger social contexts. Something is wrong somewhere, but it can no longer be seen exclusively or even primarily in the diagnosed patient."

This assertion is repeated in the manifestos of social change agents who argue that counselors and therapists should examine the institutional practices which have detrimental effects on individuals and work to change these institutions rather than counsel adjustment to the institutional dicta. Writing mainly on schizophrenia, Laing (1967) pointedly states, "The social system, and not individuals, must be the object of study if we are to understand the etiology of schizophrenia." According to this model, schizophrenia is a label applied to behavior exhibited by persons who are profoundly alienated from society. The persons labeled in this way are treated in a characteristic manner which reinforces their alienation and "symptomatic" behavior. As a means of maintaining the status quo, society then assumes the right to incarcerate such persons in mental institutions which "degrade and invalidate human beings." Treatment consists of the imposition of the therapist's or institution's perspective on the patient. Laing poses some important and as yet insufficiently answered questions about how this procedure serves to maintain the civic order and why society subscribes to these labeling and incarceration processes.

In "Rules and Metarules," a chapter within the *Politics of the Family,* Laing wryly explains about cognitive restrictions. Rules exist so that you "don't think about what you cannot think about because there is a rule against thinking about it, and a rule against thinking that there is a rule against thinking that one must not think about not thinking about certain things [p. 115]." For example, one is not supposed to think about the idea that you are not supposed to have sexual feelings about a family member because there is a rule against thinking about that thought. This is similar to many other thoughts which have to do with families, sex, and patriotism.

Mystification becomes a problem and an issue because the less we think about not thinking, the more it seems as if we never had the thoughts at all. Soon it begins to seem as if no one ever had those thoughts at all. That is, according to Laing, "by obeying a rule not to realize he is obeying a rule, he will eventually deny there is any rule he is obeying [p. 116]."

The result of all the rules and metarules is that we have squelched creativity, demanded conformity, and looked for congruence among everyone. Laing offers common examples from the school setting in which this takes place. We teach that negative attitudes are treasonous when we say, "Which one of you nice polite boys would like to hang up this coat?" (not to mention the sexist stereotyping). We engender fear of failure when a patient teacher waits and waits for a student to answer a question with hands waving around him/her so that the thought processes become paralyzed by fright even if the answer were known. When it finally is decided (by the teacher) that the student will not know the answer, the others are asked, "Who can help him/her out?" Another person achieves success, built on his/her classmate's failure. One child succeeds but one surely fails. The fear of failure however outlasts the classroom. It is learned well. It follows us through to our first job, our social relationships, our sexual relations, and our profession. (This conditioned fear of failure provides an excellent example of western socialization being harmful to humans but seldom questioned. This value is not found in American Indian cultures where individuals never achieve success at the expense of one of their tribe.)

Although the school holds many keys to the socialization process, Laing traces most of the process to the family. It is here that each of us learned whether we were good children, if what we did had an effect on others, if love was contingent on our behavior. In *Sanity, Madness and the Family* (1970), Laing and Esternsen present eleven case histories of women, mostly young, who are diagnosed schizophrenics. Extensive research into the families showed a consistent pattern of mixed messages such as "I'm always trying to get her to make more friends, but she is so self conscious. Isn't that right, dear?" Most of the patients (all were hospitalized) had gone through the good-bad-mad progression. As they strove for some measure of independence, choosing to be assertive, their parents labeled them bad. This was often in the teenage years. The next step was always to move from the bad label to the mad label. It was then only a matter of time before the process was complete. The person did in fact *act* mad.

It was found that the symptoms pointed out by the family as evidence of the person's madness often took on amazing intelligibility when viewed in terms of family interaction. Paranoid statements such as "my family is trying to poison me" might follow a period of forced medication. These families were marked by a consistent denial of the reality perceived by the patient. Each individual family member might tell the patient in private that it was the others who wanted her hospitalized.

Because problems exist and develop within families, Laing does not assume that all families will produce problems. He does assert that all families are entrusted with the task of promoting a respect for work and promoting a respect for respectability (1970). He does not, however, take the next step which many Radical Therapists would like him to take, which is to say that the structure, function and role of the family need to be examined. Radical therapists assert that problems are inherent in all families. Laing wants to examine the nexus (ties, interrelationships) of the family — those who go further assert that families as an institution cause more disadvantages than advantages. One percent of the population of the United States will at some point in their lives be diagnosed and hospitalized with the label "schizophrenic" for some behavior that troubles their relatives and friends.

Social Change Counseling considers Laing's various propositions to form a basic foundation of its theory. Although he has thus far only examined schizophrenia, it is possible that additional classifications will eventually also be traced with more assurance to the role of the environment. At any rate, there exists some social interpretation for any behavior that a person exhibits. The environment needs to be examined to determine if environmental stimuli can be altered instead of teaching adjustment to the client. We are also strongly aware of the socialization role of the family, how its values and mores are not presented as options but as truth, how labeling in and of itself produces a host of problems and perpetuates any behaviors which were previously considered undesirable, how people are taught to not think about the things which society does not want its members to think about. These and other socializations perhaps lead us to regard those who act crazy as the crazy ones. It is worth pondering that perhaps the reverse may be true.

Thomas Scheff

In an important book, *Being Mentally Ill: A Sociological Theory*, Scheff builds a case for a sociological theory of the cause of mental disorder. Beginning his discussion, the author makes a distinction between two concepts: *rule breaking* and *deviance*. "Rule breaking refers to behavior which is in clear violation of the agreed upon rules of the group . . . of social norms," whereas, "Deviance can be most usefully considered as a quality of peoples' response to an act, rather than as a characteristic of the act itself. Deviants are not a group of people who have committed the same act, but are a group of people who have been stigmatized as deviants [1966, p. 31]." By way of further definition, Scheff makes the distinction that diverse kinds of rule breaking may not have an explicit label, so sometimes the violator is labeled mentally ill. Technically this will be considered to be residual rule breaking.

To establish a sociological theory of mental illness, Scheff presents a series of hypotheses culminating in the premise that insanity exists as a social institution. Since the points which the author makes are basic to a Social Change Counseling approach, they will be reiterated here in some detail. It should be stated at this point that Scheff makes no assumption that psychiatric symptoms are rooted in underlying illness.

Scheff's first hypothesis is that residual rule breaking arises from diverse origins, such as organicity, psychological sources, external stress, and volitional acts of innovation or deviance. As such, the prevalence of unrecorded residual rule breaking is "extremely high" relative to the rate of treated mental illness. This suggests that most residual rule breaking is "denied" and is of transitory significance. Scheff states that the most important single factor in the stabilization of residual rule breaking is the societal reaction;

i.e., when the act is considered evidence of mental illness, and deviant status is accorded the rule breaker, and he or she takes on the *role* of one who is mentally ill. A perhaps isolated incident becomes the standard when the person is labeled from that one incident. In his discussion, Scheff emphasizes the involuntary aspects of role playing, noting, especially, vicarious learning as a contributory factor.

He then moves on to consider some of the beliefs and practices which make up the social institution of insanity. Even as early as childhood the stereotypical imagery surrounding mental disorder is taught. "Mental illness" becomes a frightening term, conjuring up images of crazy people laughing hysterically or engaging in bizarre and/or criminal behavior. When we say such things as "You're driving me crazy," or "You must be nuts," we are adding to this stereotype, reaffirming it inadvertently in ordinary social interaction. Media coverage and negative reports concerning mental patients and former mental patients connect violence and mental illness in addition to pointing up the supposed incurability of the disorder.

Several reasons can be given to help account for deviants' acceptance of such an unpopular role. One such reason is that deviants may be rewarded for playing the deviant role. Pressure is exerted from many sides. Psychiatrists need deviants as do other deviants. A further reason is that deviants are often punished when attempting to return to society by being subject to many forms of discrimination. In addition, during a crisis situation when rule breaking has been recognized, the deviant may find no alternative to accepting the stereotype: the role has become part of the deviant's self-concept.

Scheff continues his analysis by stating, "Among residual rule breakers, labeling is the single most important cause of careers of residual deviants [p. 92]." Most residual rule breaking is not followed by a deviant career, except in the cases in which the rule breaker becomes stereotyped. Several factors are instrumental in determining the circumstances which lead to labeling: "the degree, amount, and visibility of the rule breaking; the power of the rule breaker and the social distance between tolerance level of the community; and the availability in the culture of the community of alternative nondeviant roles [p. 96]."

A final note on Scheff's theory concerns his postulation of a deviance-amplifying system in which feedback plays an important part. It can be described as a "vicious circle begun by stigmatization, withdrawal to avoid more stigma, stigmatization because of withdrawal or its effects, and so on around the circle [p. 98]." Once labeled, the individual is caught in a downward spiral with little opportunity to interrupt this pattern. A prime concern for adherents to an activist approach to counseling and therapy is the ending of the use of psychiatric labels, calling a halt to the cycle of stigmatization before it is allowed to begin. Likewise, it is more useful to examine the social-context of behavior than to exempt society from having a role in fostering and labeling deviance.

Thomas Szasz

One of the most frequently read and most outspoken critics of the dehumanizing qualities of psychiatric practices is a psychiatrist himself, Dr. Thomas Szasz. His famous essay "The Myth of Mental Illness" can be found in a collection of essays entitled *Ideology-Insanity*. Much of the material to be presented in this discussion of Szasz's position has been gleaned from that work.

Szasz points up, very clearly, one basic postulate of a Social Change approach: that "healing acts" operate within society not outside of it. Though it is not surprising that practitioners of these acts most often reflect and promote the primary values of the society, he asserts that it is incumbent upon the practitioner to examine his/her role in promoting a covert system of ethics — what Merton might refer to as promoting a latent function of the institutional practice. The ethics involved would hardly seem covert if the client's position is looked upon, not in a traditional manner, but in the way in which Szasz sums up the course of "psychiatric events."

> We regard the rich and influential psychiatric patient as a self-governing, responsible client — free to decide whether or not to be a patient. But we look upon the poor and the aged patient as a ward of the state, too ignorant or too "mentally sick" to know what is best for him. The paternalistic psychiatrist, as an agent of the family or the state, assumes "responsibility" for him, defines him as a "patient" against his will and subjects him to treatment deemed best for him, with or without his consent [1970, p. 86].

Using strong words, Szasz contends that the concept of mental illness is a totalitarian one in which one person is permitted to impose his/her will on another. He continues by saying that in the United States, when the ideology of totalitarianism is promoted in terms of communism or facism, it is rejected. However, when promoted under the banner of "mental health," totalitarianism is embraced wholeheartedly. Under the guise of "mental health" justification is found for a feudal kind of subjugation.

Szasz also discusses the mental health ethic from a legal standpoint. He sees both psychiatry and the law concerned with determining the social legitimacy of various roles, and also with enforcing conformity to these roles. "Institutional psychiatry enforces role conformity by defining role deviance as mental illness punishable by committtment [1970, p. 102]." He poses the question, "Why isn't all socially undesirable behavior proscribed by law and punished by penal sanctions? And why isn't all other conduct allowed [1970, p. 102]?" To expand upon this point, why is it that society has created two institutions to limit socially undesirable behavior and enforce role conformity? Is deviance so threatening to our society to require so much effort to bring it under control? The loss of liberty imposed by involuntary psychiatric hospitalization is one of the most severe penalties that the legal system has the power to bring down upon a human being. In this sense, most psychiatric institutions function as prisons to which individuals can involuntarily be committed with indefinite sentences. Especially in areas where there is no death penalty, it is important to scrutinize discussions of criminal responsibility in this light. Relegation to an institution becomes a life sentence.

Thomas Szasz is perhaps most famous for his conceptualization of the "myth of mental illness." In brief, his assertion is that the function of mental illness is to disguise the existence of moral conflicts in human relations. The illness myth diverts attention from a confrontation with ethical, political, and social values to a more ambiguous inner dynamic of psychopathology. Szasz prefers to use the term "problem in living" for deviation from psychosocial or ethical standards rather than the medical term "mental illness" which connotes some type of personality or brain dysfunction. His aim is to encourage a new look at what is called "mental illness" by removing it from the illness category and regarding it as the "expression of man's struggle with the problem of how he should live [1970, p. 21]," a problem which reflects both his inability to cope with his environment and his increasing self-reflectiveness. It is this concept of the myth of mental illness which has made Thomas Szasz such an important figure in modern day psychiatry and psychology and which has sparked the interest of many others who question the assumptions behind many types of therapy.

Seymour Halleck

Halleck has written several books and papers dealing with the need for psychiatric reform, the most popular being his recent work, *The Politics of Therapy* (1967), which will be discussed here. Throughout this book Halleck points to the need for psychiatrists (and all others dealing with psychological concerns) to become aware of their political roles and to take responsibility for the political effects of their therapeutic interventions. He states that there is no such position as that of psychiatric neutrality and that any encounter with a psychiatrist has political implications. The role of the mental health professional can no longer be viewed in terms of the interactions with a client. Once the professional is aware of the political impact of his/her work, this role must be evaluated in terms of the impact it holds for the social system. Those who think that only the client is affected by psychological intervention are wearing blinders which filter out the social and political aspects of human existence. Regardless of motivation or intention, by reinforcing those in power, the professional is committing a political act; by failing to encourage a client to examine or confront the environment, the professional has made a contribution to the strengthening of the status quo. It is only by emphasizing the oppressiveness of the client's external environment or by showing the client how to change that environment that the mental health professional facilitates an altering of the status quo. One can either encourage a client to accept the existing distribution of power or encourage him/her to change it. This is, to Halleck, the essence of the political nature of therapy. By working with those who at times seem handicapped, the therapist comes to view human unhappiness as a product of individual disorder, carrying the assumption that the institutions that affect the individual are more or less adequate. Halleck attacks the fallacy that the source of the problem lies within the individual, and the institutions which are supposed to serve the individual are for all practical purposes above reproach. He also points out that when individuals attempt to solve their problems by changing something about themselves, they are distracted from dealing with the external environment. Therapy, which fosters a preoccupation with internal problems, promotes activity on the part of the client which will not be directed toward confronting social systems. If a client is focusing on an internal state, he/she will not be working to change the external state.

In *The Politics of Therapy,* Halleck contends that much of environmental stress on individuals is brought on by society's failure to satisfy some of the basic psychological needs of its members. Despite, or because of, the intentions of its creators and maintainers, society may take on an oppressiveness of its own. "Subtle prejudices, outmoded and inflexible rules, and demands imposed by a particular economic system may become potent stresses by depriving large numbers of citizens of the basic human needs [p. 8]." In the opinion of the authors, the social system should certainly be questioned regarding the effects it has on individuals and groups. Systems and institutions are not always without fault. If the stress emanating from the oppressiveness of the social system is direct, the individual may be able to locate the source of that stress. If, however, the stress is of an indirect nature, the source may not be so easily found. Those individuals who are subject to indirect stress of unknown origin are more likely to believe that the source of the problem lies within themselves and to hold themselves to blame because they cannot find any other reason for their problem. It is these individuals who either ask or are told to change their behavior, because the problem is theirs not society's. One is left in a most vulnerable position when forced to look at a problem as a function of stress coming totally from within rather than from without.

According to Halleck, a client's ability to change an oppressive environment is dependent upon three different contingencies: his/her psychological strength; an awareness of what the environment is doing to him/her; and motivation to change the environment. Given ability in all three of these areas, the person must also know how to make an evaluation of what about the environment is worth changing. Individual psychotherapy, as it is practiced today, fosters adjustment to the environment and does not offer the client the alternative of changing his/her circumstances. Activism has never been a goal of therapy. To Halleck, however, activism can certainly be a legitimate end product of psychological intervention with a client, since therapy need not and should not be a "handmaiden of the status quo."

The Radical Therapy Movement

Perhaps the most outspoken and most revolutionary of all the groups calling for a change in the adjustment notion of therapy is a group once known as the Radical Therapy (RT) Collective, and later comprising the staff of *Rough Times*. Their motto is, "Therapy means change not adjustment." The Collective includes in its ranks radical therapists, feminists, members of gay liberation, and representatives of the Insane Liberation Front. All of these groups are in some way concerned with the political nature of therapy and the need for changing the oppressive nature of many institutions within the social structure.

According to its proponents, RT is not a new kind of therapy but a way of living. It starts from "the awareness that therapy is a social and political event, and moves to the conviction that therapy systems — like many of this country's institutions — must be changed [Agel, 1971, p. ix]." Claude Steiner, who is involved in the RT movement, has written a "Radical Psychiatry Manifesto" in which he proclaims that individual psychotherapy is elitist, outmoded, and nonproductive. It reinforces the idea that people's difficulties are rooted within themselves, while implying that the world about us is functioning well. Therapy also encourages secrecy and shame and is thereby oppressive. Steiner points to what other writers have also said, that by supposedly remaining neutral, psychiatrists and others have actually come to enforce established values and laws. In the manifesto, he relates some new and controversial definitions of psychiatric nomenclature.

> Paranoia is a state of heightened awareness. . . . Depression is the result of alienation of human from human. Violent anger is a healthy reaction to oppression. Drug abuse is taught to children by their alcholic, nicotinic, aspirinic elders. Schizophrenia is an experience saner than "normality" in this mad world. . . . Psychiatric deception of the oppressed is at the root of people's alienation [Agel, 1971, pp. xv–xxiii].

It is likely that many in the mental health professions will find Steiner's words to be too caustic or may say that he is delusional himself. The point in quoting this material is that the profession cannot ignore such critics. Others in addition to Steiner are questioning the assumptions and the goals of the therapeutic process.

RT calls for an end to the mystification of therapist role, which has made practitioners a privileged elite, accountable to no one. It is the skill of the therapist that is useful, not the role. Therapy today is a power relationship between people — one up, one down. It embodies the problem of our society rather than offering a viable solution. Therapy can help only those who adhere to the system and who wish to maintain their place in it. The work of the radical therapist involves a considerable amount of risk-taking in organizing clients and mental health workers and in attacking some of society's sacred institutions.

Radical therapy is founded on several principles. One principle is that in the absence of oppression (defined here as coercion by force or threats of force), human beings can live in harmony with themselves and with nature. Alienation is the result of oppression, and is at the root of all psychological problems. Those oppressed are deceived into believing either that they are not oppressed, or that there are good reasons behind their oppression. RT should be practiced in groups to give the alienated individual contact and support. Several formulae are presented which summarize the theory:

> Oppression + Deception = Alienation
> Oppression + Awareness = Anger
> Contact + Awareness = Liberation
> [Agel, 1971]

The first formula describes the condition in which most people live. They are oppressed but are mystified and deceived about that oppression. They consequently feel it is their own fault. The result is alienation. When people become aware of their oppression and deception, anger results. This is the current status of many members of liberation groups — women, gay, black, Indian.

The third formula is *Contact + Awareness = Liberation.* By making contact with others who are also oppressed the anger can be channeled and used. Frantz Fanon, in *The Wretched of the Earth* (1968), his classic work about oppressed peoples in Algeria under the French colonization, noted that a large dose of revolution was the key to many problems he found in his psychiatric office.

The Radical Therapy movement continues to grow in strength and number and the views of its proponents are having increasing impact. The Social Change approach joins with the Radical Therapy movement in looking at the role of culture in people's problems, and in examining the notion that our goal of "mental health" may never be accomplished because our socialization is producing problems faster than they can be countered. It is also possible that the basic counseling relationship may be counterproductive to people helping each other. These are issues which cannot be resolved without further thought and research. It is clear, however, that questions about the effect of societal variables and the nature of counseling do exist.

2

Assumptions of the Theory

This chapter will focus on the nature of humans, the conditions of their existence, their adaptations to stress and anxiety, and their use of symptoms and deviance as means of coping with living conditions. Counselors' ideas and beliefs about people greatly affect the way in which they perceive their clients, the acceptable manners of interaction, and the methods and strategies that are deemed appropriate. Therefore, a look at the human condition is essential before considering the manner and means of practicing Social Change Counseling.

The first section of this chapter deals with the nature of humans; those attributes of individuals which the authors believe to be common to all members of American society. The next section moves to a discussion of the human condition; the environmental stimuli which impinge on all people as a result of their existence as social animals. The final two sections reflect on symptomatology and deviance, their etiology, uses and abuses.

Nature of Humans

The common attributes of all individuals within this culture include the political nature of humans, "limited" free will, roles, intimacy, and the effects of change and hope.

The Political Nature of Humans

Aristotle has said that "man is by nature a political animal [McKeon, 1941, p. 1129]." This is borne out by the array of governments and controlling systems which have colored human history. The authors have adopted Millett's (1969, p. 23) definition of politics for use in this context.

> "Politics" shall refer to power-structured arrangements whereby one group of persons is controlled by another. . . although an ideal politics might simply be conceived of as the arrangement of human life on agreeable and rational principles, from whence the entire notion of power *over* others should be banished . . . this is not what constitutes the political as we know it.

Whenever two or more persons have joined in business, love, or a community for mutual gain, basic rules, structures, and power relationships have overtly or covertly been established. The assertion that this characteristic has been socialized by cultures across time will be presented here briefly.

Those advocating a socialization theory suggest that the political attribute is learned in the primary (extended or surrogate) family. Everyone is first educated within these basic structures during early learning years. Children learn of the tendency to establish power relationships by viewing their parents (or their substitutes) from positions of dependency. A conceptualization of the way the world functions falls into a power/powerless dichotomy. Reinforcement of this early learning occurs in the next significant encounter which children make: schools. Teachers hold power over students who must follow lest they suffer when grades are given. Because everyone is born into a position of powerlessness (i.e., infancy), no one escapes the learning.

A variation of the family-learning socialization premise is the assertion that the search for power is a learned response to any culture which values and rewards potency, domination, and strength. This may be seen in a capitalistic society or any other system which chooses its leaders according to power criteria.

Whether the behavior is learned or innate, "man is political." Taken broadly this means that individuals have a need to feel they are influential (superior, powerful and/or stronger than their opponents). When threatened or violated, a common response is aggressive behavior. Because individuals (or groups or nations) so often feel insecure, controls and constraints are imposed upon the weakest by the strongest in an attempt to prevent possible future threats. The means of guarding against threat include governmental systems with laws which try to limit and control the actions or power of individuals and moral codes which also establish rules for behavior.

Capacity for Free Will

The second human characteristic which will be discussed is the capacity for free will. Perhaps no other trait has been so widely disputed and defended. Social Change Counseling takes neither the position that humans have free choice or that they are bound to respond to whatever stimuli have been conditioned. Rather, it supports the notion that we do have choices among alternatives, but these alternatives have been greatly reduced by the boundaries of society's values and ethics. These limits are sometimes codified into law (e.g., prohibiting adultery, homosexuality) but often are only supported by social values and public opinion (e.g., nuclear families, having children, going to college, buying new cars, etc.). Whether written or unwritten, these "laws" result in a limiting of options for anyone who values, desires, or seeks the support or approval of his/her culture.

In these ideas, Social Change Counseling allys itself with early Radical Therapy advocates, Claude Steiner and Hogie Wycoff. In an adaptation of Transactional Analysis, Steiner pointed out the stroke economy of our culture. Because "strokes" (positive human recognition) are considered essential to human happiness, those who are stroke givers (initially parents) are in a position of extreme power. Parents, and later others, are able to control behavior, by regulating a constant state of stroke deprivation.

This deprivation keeps everyone in a constant search for approval (or strokes) and therefore in their appropriate role. Our roles vary by age, sex, socioeconomic class and geographic region but essentially constitute an established way of behaving which does not alter the status quo. Our culture provides strokes for all who are like everyone else or just a little better. Someone who "marches to a different drummer," however, rarely receives the commendation of his/her peers. This may seem far afield from the free will issue as it is usually discussed, but is intended to shed a different light on the assumption that individuals have the capability or capacity to be free choosing. Because people desire the approval of others and because that approval is so conditionally given (we do not regard all others with unconditional positive regard), controls are established which weed out deviance, difference, and divergence. Man's insecurity and uncertainty is rooted in the conditionality of approval and the controls which it engenders.

Some do manage to be different. This produces dissonance, and the culture has developed means to maintain the status quo and to reduce this dissonance. For those for whom approval is not sufficiently motivating, society provides mental institutions, labels, prisons, and deprivation of privileges (e.g., no recess for talking during class). It would be difficult to isolate the effects of desire for approval and fear of culture's power to maintain conformity. Together, however, they produce a force strong enough to subdue each person's desire to be a free agent; they give us our orderly acquiescent society.

Desire for Approval

By inference, our third characteristic of the human condition is the desire for approval, strokes or blessing. The result of this search for others' acceptance and esteem is a reduction in deviance and the maintenance of the status quo. As the drive for homogeneity continues so does the current norm. Conformity is reinforced in a number of ways, a few include: 1) the push by parents for their children's acceptance by others culminating in the popularity contests of junior high and high school; 2) the cumulative school folder in which any deviance is recorded, which follows a student through his/her academic career; 3) the bestowing of teacher or parental approval (and therefore favors) to the children who conform and cause the fewest problems; 4) the media — when you act like the television family and dress like the magazines, you will be happy; and 5) the advertising industry — if you buy the right products all the best things in life will be yours.

Human insecurity breeds the constant search for approval. Because approval is most often contingent upon conformity, except in extreme cases, conformity is assured. The individual is taught to believe if two companions say they like a movie, it is best to agree lest he/she be thought to have poor taste, or if a group of students are complaining about a teacher's strictness, the one student who appreciates the learning dares not speak out for the teacher lest he/she be branded the teacher's pet. In essence the lesson to all is conform so that approval can be gained, or at least disapproval can be avoided.

Roles

A basic facet of each person is the role he/she plays. A role is essentially the "pattern of behavior regularly utilized by individuals who occupy a social status, is part of the personality [Honigman, 1967, p. 131]." The culture in which everyone learns and grows includes and teaches many standardizations of behavior. Some of the basic ideas which are taught to all are to be on time, to get along with other people, and to produce and consume prodigiously. Also conditioned less obtrusively, but nevertheless systematically, is the idea concerning the powerlessness of individuals being related to their material possessions. For example, rich people are always in the news, therefore what they do is more important than what an average citizen does.

The above ideas form the general characteristics of the role of a "good person." Beyond that, roles become very specialized to fit any combination of race, sex, social class, age, schooling, employment and place of residence.

A role is essentially a collection of behaviors which are imitated in order to achieve the somewhat illusory sense of belonging that accompanies fitting the norm. Knowing one's role eliminates decisions about how to act or feel about everyday happenings; the role specifies them. Consequently, a role eases the tension and uncertainty which would accompany deciding for oneself. There is comfort in knowing that by following the rules, rewards can be anticipated.

There are times, however, when these roles are not beneficial. Roles also produce conflict when two parts of a person's role are in opposition. A teenager certainly experiences this conflict when his/her obedient child role and role as a peer do not agree. Likewise, a male worker faces a difficult decision when his compliant worker-role and his good-provider-role are conflicted as the workers contemplate unionization.

On the basis of what has been stated, however, it could easily be said roles are generally more helpful than harmful: they take care of incidental decisions, they are troubled only when important decisions need to be made, they provide stability in our culture. Unfortunately they have another component: they impose certain limitations. Referring back to the criteria which specify a person's role (race, age, sex, social class, schooling, and residence), differences clearly exist between what is appropriate for some people to do and what is inappropriate for others to do. For example, many older citizens cannot work after age 65, and families feel that constant vigilence must be given to older family members in order to take care of them. It is appropriate to go to college and find a career when you are 18, but a person who starts college at age 35 is frowned upon. Sex also provides limits. Children read in school books about girls who are weak and always call on boys to solve their problems. The message is explicit that girls do not take care of themselves, and boys know the right answers to problems. Young women graduating from college are constricted by their sex role when employers ask them their plans for marriage and family. The same is seldom discussed in their male counterparts' interviews. Furthermore, women are essentially damned by either possible answer to the marriage and family question: a "no" says something is wrong with you, while a "yes" eliminates one from the competition as a poor employment risk.

The same kinds of examples are easily found for the other criteria of race, schooling, residence and class. It is sometimes thought that vast progress has been made in the elimination of role stereotyping. The various liberation movements have certainly begun that long struggle. It is true, nevertheless, that the vast majority of the population are untouched by any changes or are disdainful of the ones they see. These severe restrictions and limitations which are imposed upon all people constitute the oppressive aspects of roles in our society. This imposition is at the expense of all the persons whose wishes and desires lie outside their assigned roles.

Roles also maintain the status quo. No rapid changes are possible when everyone has learned through similar systems. Maintenance of the status quo is frequently debated with equal fervor as desirable or undesirable. Evidence such as "western cultures have more goods and resources than anyone else ever in history" is used as the rationale that our current situation should be maintained. The counter position is simply that the existence we have does have more goods and benefits, but humans are still hurting, anxious, depressed, angry, and guilty, sometimes in direct response to the goods which are supposed to make them happy. The potential rewards are great for seeking a different mode of operating, a different culture, and a less constricting set of values which may allow more people to feel better through greater personal freedom.

In summary, roles are a collection of learnings which form a pattern of behavior. These patterns are helpful to individuals at times because they alleviate many small decisions and provide a sense of stability which might be hard to achieve without much standardization. They are detrimental to a person because they limit the options which are available and are detrimental to society's progress because they maintain the status quo.

Intimacy

The problems which beset the clients of the many mental health facilities in schools and communities frequently contain a component which deals with intimacy and relations with other humans.

Those who do not have close relationships would like to achieve some measure of intimacy, those who are involved in intimate relationships have trouble handling the ramifications and accompanying emotions. Perhaps no other facet of the human condition provides as much stress. It is likely that our early conditioning dictates many of our feelings about intimacy since most humans are initially cared for in an intimate way. Animal research on contact deprivation suggests that severe maladjustment may result from continued deprivation.

Much of a person's intimacy is usually found within the ceremonial and blood relationships of the family or marriage. For that reason, strengthening the family unit may possess some validity. It is possible, however, that family relationships have been given permission in our society to contain intimacy. If that permission were extended to other types of relationships, intimacy might be more readily available to those who do not, by choice or default, have a family.

Social Change Counseling maintains that the present condition of our society and culture prevents many possible expressions of intimacy. Restricting close relationships only to those encompassed by the family circle is one way in which expressions of intimacy are constricted. There are many other instances of cultural and societal restrictions. For example, in reference to the previous section on roles, we find that sex, age, race, class, schooling and residence provide subtle and explicit restrictions on the types of relationships which are socially, or morally acceptable for each group. A relationship between two homosexuals, an interracial couple, or a friendship that crosses social class lines do not receive support and commendation in our society as do those relationships which remain within the rules. Upon examination, it is hard to support those restrictions.

Beyond role restrictions our culture makes close relationships difficult to obtain because of some of its values. Competition is taught in western cultures from infancy through retirement and certainly constrains possible friendly feelings. When winning is valued so highly, the message to also be friends is received rather weakly by young scholars and athletes. High need for achievement, which is likewise often taught in large doses to young people, is not conducive to the development of honest open relationships.

Additionally, the emphasis on the difference between males and females causes restrictions inhibiting possible closer relationships. Girls who are taught that securing a husband is a major goal in life certainly narrow their field of prospective relationships. Similarly, as boys are socialized to be brave and strong, to know how to handle situations, and to have a career that will support a wife and family, they too are limited in the type and nature of relationships which will be acceptable. Friendships between males frequently will not contain a strong feeling component because it is thought inappropriate or feminine.

Lastly, our culture supports a privacy value which is largely contradictory to the intimacy which most desire. We are taught to keep children from telling family secrets, not to share weaknesses, and to wait some appropriate amount of time before sharing important information with an acquaintance. The message is to resist intimate discussions.

It seems that intimacy is highly valued by humans. It constitutes a major problem area for those persons who do not have the close relationships they desire and those who are involved in close relationships which produce undesired complications. These problems are largely due to the values and restrictions which are taught within our culture. These values specify what relationships are and are not appropriate and limit the achievement of close relationships with other people.

Constancy and Change

The human being presents a confusing picture on the issue of change and constancy. The process of living implies continuous change in the psychological, biological, and cognitive domains. As we grow older our bodies change, our feelings and awarenesses change, and we acquire new intellectual information and insights. The rate of growth is most rapid during the early years and reaches a plateau in early adulthood. It is at this point that conflict arises. Many actions of adults indicate a desire to maintain the present, hold fast to that which already is. Examples of this are the great amount of ambivalence one experiences when trying to make such decisions as changing jobs, leaving a marriage, or trading in an old, trusty piece of clothing for a replacement.

Conversely, creative and cultural achievements, inventions, and the thousands of other changes which have occurred in any single life span surely attest to the capacity, even desire for changes which are perceived as beneficial. It seems, however, that we have not found an ideal rate of change which keeps pace with desires and allows for personal adjustment. Alvin Toffler in *Future Shock* (1970) identifies four coping behavior styles used when change is too rapid. The Denier, the Specialist, the Reversionist and the Super Simplifier each have a unique manner of sorting, blocking and classifying change which happens too quickly.

Upon closer examination, it is generally seen that most changes are those which are external to individuals: changes in styles, changes in jobs, changes in ways to spend time. Far fewer result in changes of a person's perceptions of the world, style of coping, or feelings about him/herself. Toffler offers the explanation that the psychological and physiological structure can only tolerate a given (although unknown) amount of change and the resultant stress without experiencing "future shock." Most people develop a defense against too much change. For example, a person who changes jobs every few years may have a very stable home and familial relationship and may maintain mostly friends from college. A person who is constantly looking for excitement and diversity in one part of his/her life by drifting in and out of many relationships, may regiment his/her daily routine and occupation such that they are not overstimulated.

Putting this all together, it is possible that because so many things are happening and fluctuating in our world and environment, it is nearly impossible or undesirable for individuals to consciously or unconsciously seek change within themselves. The body has built-in protection against that much stimulation. Consequently, humans are essentially unadvanced in the realms of knowing themselves, understanding personal relationships, and interpreting human behavior. Our social sciences have not received the attention of most other areas because of self-protection.

This explanation is consistent with the cry for simplicity — back to the earth and the good old days — which is uttered by young and old alike. A recent popular song appealed to all who would hear to "Slow down, you move too fast; got to make the morning last." The predicted result of this, from the songwriter, is to "feel groovy."

Hope and Religion

It appears from reflection on the cultures which have come and gone over the centuries that in each there has been some search for an entity, an idea, a god which would explain why things are as they are, and to give a reason for this existence. As with other areas of human existence, little progress has been made in all the years of trying. Two explanations for the search come to mind. First, that the human condition is meaningless and therefore humans invent gods and reasons for existence. The religious explanation is that a god does exist and he contacts people on earth to help them through awareness of a spiritual being. Whichever explanation is the truth, humans are often in a position to seek a meaning which transcends this existence. The position of a Social Change Counseling approach is that such activity may be helpful and is an alternative that is available for those who choose to use it.

However, the status of religion is such that it has become one of the institutions of our culture. It carries power in the form of political influence, guilt infliction, and threats to the nonconformists. Religion has become a tool of our culture and one of the methods by which our culture limits the alternatives and options of its members. Through the doctrine which is largely established by an elite (if not the elite of today, then the elite of another age who passed it to the elite of the next generation), "good" (conforming) behavior is rewarded with promises for eternal life and "bad" (nonconforming) behavior is limited through threats of disapproval or eternal suffering. As such, organized religion exhibits a sharp difference between the latent and manifest functions described by Thomas Merton. The manifest function of religion is to make individuals feel better, directly and indirectly by attempting to explain the chaotic existence of humanity. On the other hand the latent function of religion maintains considerable power for controlling the behavior of a society that may not have even committed itself to a religious ethic.

The Human Condition

The human condition is the term used by the authors to refer to the elements which surround our daily lives; forces which are outside the individual and largely beyond his/her control. Within this area we consider the social character of America, the role of families in socializing dependency and powerlessness, and the oppression and anxiety which has developed en masse from the meaningless work of the industrial age.

To accept the task of writing about what it is like to live in a contemporary western society first means accepting the fact that generalizations must be made. It is impossible to make statements which will describe the idealized middle-class family in which family members love each other, communicate, enjoy their particular occupations and have a happy life, and simultaneously describe the stereotypical broken home where children run the streets, physical force is used for discipline, and no one ever knows or cares about the feelings of the others. It is equally difficult to find the commonalities across social classes, geographic regions and ethnic groups.

Social Character

In spite of the vast differences, the authors believe there does exist a common core, a standard set of teachings and values which are basic to the American culture. Some of these values are taught in the public schools under an umbrella heading like "good citizenship." These values are also learned through the media as "typical" families, their doctors, their friends and relatives are portrayed to all who watch them live their "normal" days. From these television shows (also literature, and newspapers to a lesser extent) the rules of our culture are portrayed in living color: "Boys don't like to cook"; "Girls don't play football"; "You should spend your money on the newest, biggest and best anything"; "If you smoke cigarettes, drink diet pop, drive a sports car, and brush your teeth with Brand Z, you will soon have a beautiful member of the opposite sex at your side."

To a ghetto child we teach middle-class values even though that child may never live in an environment in which these values will be appropriate. We teach strict sex role behavior (children's readers are often the worst offenders) even though our society clearly presents many examples of individuals who deviate from those rules who are happy and well functioning. We have the erroneous belief that until people are at least teenagers it is inappropriate to deal with ethics and differing ways of handling the situations of living. Until that time, only one way, one approach, one solution is presented by the family and school. By the time the student reaches the "appropriate" time for him/her to think about choices, his/her life has already been programmed. Is it any wonder that a high school course in civics could hardly conduct a discussion of the problems of democracy? That is one of the things about which we have rules not to think about thinking.

This central core of teachings provides many of the limits of free choice which were previously mentioned under roles. These general teachings are the foundation of the American culture, the social milieu of the United States. We need to stop and consider how high a price we are willing to pay for that commonality. How expensive is homogeneity and lack of deviance?

Erich Fromm calls the results of the socialization the "social character." He identifies values such as punctuality, productivity, consumption and getting along with others as parts of that social character. If we identify our social system as a network of positions and statuses, each with a built-in, expected role, this system develops into a force in and of itself. The force strives to maintain itself. Everyone must perform his/her role in order for the SYSTEM to continue functioning. The SYSTEM shapes humans to conform to its needs. These needs are translated into expectations, rules, and rewards which are inculcated into everyone from the nursery onward.

Some reject this apparent personification of our social system, maintaining that it has no movement and is only a product of the people who comprise it. They contend it is foolish to think of a system as having a will and power of its own. Perhaps all those things are true. However, a certain force operates which defies logic, such that projects in which people have lost interest are continued — just because they were already begun, just because we have already spent so much money, just because it "must" be finished. In the name of progress, roads are constructed for which no one can identify a need (e.g. the "Bridge to Nowhere" in Pittsburgh). Courses are taught and no one seems to know anymore why that subject matter is still included in the curriculum. Whether we personify the force which keeps the world moving in the same direction, or whether we call it inertia, or maintenance of the status quo, there is an effect of things-are-the-way-they-are-because they-have-always-been-and-therefore-this-is-the-proper-way-to-do-things. Through guilt, criticism, punishment for failure and other such "negative sanctions," the social system prevents most deviance from continuing or recurring (Honigman, 1967, p. 131). Further, it is important to recognize the interrelationship of culture and personality. They simultaneously influence each other. This is very analogous to B. F. Skinner's notion that the environment and people are simultaneously changing each other in a circular system. This represents the evolutionary theory of social change which is very slow and unresponsive.

A variation of this theory is the revitalization theory suggested by Honigman (1967). When a society, culture or situation becomes too oppressive, a leader appears to help the people change some aspect of their current life. The changes which are effected are then institutionalized; they become the norm. They then form the situation which causes stress for others, and the cycle is restarted. Because this is always a reactive stance, this philosophy or orientation will never succeed in actually catching-up, or alleviating the strife which causes revolution. This always-behind-the-times socialization has been an age-old plague visited on humans throughout recorded history. For this reason, some assert that it is part of human nature. We maintain that it is the result of lack of planning and foresight. Like the crowded, narrow streets in older cities, outdated values are attributed to human nature because that-is-the-way-it-used-to-be-done. No one finds the streets "wrong" because technology now plans differently to meet the needs of today. Because our socialization has always been for the generation behind us, does not mean that it cannot be changed. Children could be taught to live for the world into which they are growing.

An activist approach to counseling maintains that psychology has been a primary force in maintaining this generation lag during recent decades. Psychology is used as an explanation of what everyone already believes. Cloaked in the assurance that science "proved" it, human nature is described. When studying human subjects, the culture is a confounding variable that is always present yet never acknowledged. Studies can "prove" that female and male children play differently, think differently, act differently; they can prove that differences really do exist between races or ethnic groups; they can prove that alienated youth place a higher value on pleasure than work. These studies are given with the intention of describing real differences. One is easily caught up in believing these results without taking the next step and examining the causes of the differences. No one has raised a male child as a female or vice-versa to know the effects of socialization vs. hormones. No Chicano could erase a personal history as a Chicano to repeat those same years as a WASP. These are obvious examples of how psychology has theorized and proven to the public what humans are like. We contend that psychology is merely a reflection of the socialization. It reports what has happened while purporting to explain basic differences.

Families

Moving to the particular, we will first examine the human condition within a family. Being born into a family or surrogate family is a condition, role or situation which no one escapes. If a nuclear or substitute family is not the initial agent, another institution, whether foster family or orphanage, is responsible for the initial care of each child. The role of infant and child socializes some very distinct attributes into everyone. First and foremost from the child's helpless position he/she learns the meaning of powerlessness. Not having a voice in deciding when the family moves, when to play and when to sleep, or when to buy something in a store, makes it obvious to a youngster that others, mainly adults, control the world, and especially his/her world. We do not mean to assert that control and guidance is not required for young children; we are only describing the effect of that one-down position. This state of affairs is not changed when the youngster faces the next primary contact — school. Many may find this even more controlling than the life to which they were accustomed at home. We will pick up later on the result of this powerless feeling.

Another attribute of families is the socialized interdependency. Children are told, "If you do not pick up your toys it makes Mommie feel bad"; or, "Let's both go outside and have fun."

Somehow one's actions are inextricably tied to another's feelings. Somehow one is then responsible for how someone else feels. Family members are ashamed or proud of something another sibling or family member does. This reciprocal concern and interdependency soon becomes a right: one person of a group is not supposed to do things that will give others bad feelings; everyone is supposed to make others feel good. No one stops to question why one's emotions are intertwined with others'.

This process is crucial to the building of the "Us and Them dichotomy" (Laing, 1972). It is the Us and Them psychology which shores up one nation to fight another nation, which defines and splits the brotherhood of mankind so that one portion of it may be killed or despised for the sake of protecting "us." What "they" think becomes a crucial force for determining how "we" will live. "What will others think" keeps boys and girls from disobeying their parents. It keeps everyone buying new clothes and cars because "what would people think if I were out of style?" One group of people becomes powerful and able to motivate a different group if the latter can be defined as "them." North Vietnam was not a problem for Americans until it was defined as "them," which was the opposite of "us."

Today's families are seldom extended as they were in the past. They normally consist of one or two parents and one to three children. Uncles, aunts, grandparents and cousins may live thousands of miles away and are known only through a yearly vacation and a holiday telephone call. This phenomenon is widely discussed in contemporary psychology and sociology. Seldom included in these discussions is the pressure that results from having access to fewer people. That is, there are fewer people and consequently everyone must assume more roles. With fewer available family members (with whom permission is given to be close) fewer alliances and friendships result. One is left with fewer alternatives.

First, consider the unavailability of people for the many roles needed in a home. Roles, or duties, such as gardener, fix-it person, always-ready-for-a-laugh person, good-to-talk-seriously-with person, plus all the usual attending aspects of mother, father, son, and daughter must be assumed. It is likely that every family will not have a willing volunteer for such tasks and roles; someone must assume a role unwillingly or the position is left vacant. Either alternative provides a strain on the daily working relationships in a family. This is closely tied to the second ramification of small family groups: few alternatives for alliances. Because the relationships which exist among family members contain permission which no other relationship can equal, it is possible that persons will go through life without the friendships and alliances which might have been possible if they had known more of their relatives. Few know the joys of the grandparent-grandchild duo, complete with stories which make a different time in history come alive. Not many contemporary persons experience their siblings in an adult relationship. Most have only holiday contacts following high school.

David Cooper in "Being Born Into a Family" (Brown, ed., 1974), developed the ideas of our social interdependency in the family and the lack of choice of roles which are available to each new sibling. First, people are glued together because each has been taught that a person is incomplete as a singleton. Thus a family tries to fill the missing part with a child. If that child succeeds in leaving his/her parents, the child will also feel incomplete, alone. The cycle is restarted with each generation. Additionally, each child is indoctrinated from birth onward regarding the kind of son or daughter the parents wish their child to grow up to be. Indoctrination comes quickly regarding the kind of husband or wife which would be acceptable. Everyone is taught, that he/she should look for a mate who is "normal" in every respect, even though their personal needs might best be met by someone who is very much not normal.

Most families teach stricter rules than would be required to get along in society. The creativity, dreams, and spontaneity of each person are replaced with etiquette, organized games, and mechanized learning. When children play, they seldom create and devise new approaches. If they play school, it is a mirror image of how school really is; likewise house, cowboys, or train. Unfortunately adults cannot even tell them to use their own "secret wisdom" which they have been taught to forget, because adults have forgotten that they have forgotten it (Cooper, in Brown, ed. 1974).

Cultural Artifacts

Adults in contemporary society reflect those things which they learned as children. Most adults still feel powerless. Halleck (1971) asserts that an individual's quest for power is inversely related to the belief regarding his/her own capacity to have influence. If that relationship is true, it is clear that people do not feel they have much influence, for the greater part of people's lives are spent in trying to gain a job which will give them more authority, and in living in human relationships in which there is a constant struggle for control. History provides many examples of men and women who have made their life goals the accumulation of power and influence.

Most adults are also anxious. A contemporary writer was recently quoted as saying that, in order to sell his novels, he only had to write stories which would allow already present anxiety to be displaced onto his books, and the public would love it. This anxiety is the result of many factors, primarily the conflict of individual nature vs. the roles one is expected to enact. That is, the wants vs. the shoulds. Freudian psychology based much of its philosophy on the controlling of human impulses. People have been trying to accomplish that goal for decades. It is worth questioning what the advantages of this perpetual control are, since a nation of anxious individuals is the result. Ulcers, migraine headaches, upset stomachs and hundreds of other physical manifestations of anxiety can be found. Halleck contends that we are alienated from our true selves to such an extent that our divided and fragmented selves produce this anxiety and ontological guilt.

We are alienated from our thoughts as a result of our lack of opportunity to think and question. We are alienated from our emotions because of the strict rules about what one should feel in various situations. We are alienated from our bodies because sexual and sensual feelings are mystified and controlled. We are alienated from our work because we do not have direct influence on the products we make or their distribution. There is little left in our lives which can truly be said to be a product of our personhood. Dreams are one source of our person. Most dreams, however, are viewed as strange and unintelligible. Perhaps that reflects how out of touch with ourselves we really are.

People in America are oppressed and controlled by many forces and influences. This becomes a problem in that most believe it is just and natural for them to be in that position. As long as it is defined in that way, freedom will not exist. If women, blacks, students, and any other oppressed groups maintain that others really are superior, the situation has no chance of changing. It is only through awareness that the status quo can be altered. Erich Fromm (1955) includes a spurious sense of freedom as a part of the "social character." While believing in individual autonomy, anonymous authorities are commanding one's existence.

The industrial age has produced a culture of sameness. Suburbs, television shows, cigarettes, magazines and cake mixes each vary little from one brand to another. However, each wages million-dollar campaigns to profess its individuality. Additionally, we have become a throw-away temporary society. Get-away weekends, disposable food containers, temporary classrooms, paper and plastic dishes, and paper dresses are all signs of the transient for-the-moment ethic which pervades our every-day living. It is hard to estimate the effect of this nonpermanence. *Future Shock* (Toffler, 1970) provided a best-selling warning for us to slow down or at least maintain some personal and national stability. It appears, however, that the pace and progress at which we travel has gathered its own momentum and will not be slowing down for those who may have trouble at the present pace.

Throughout this section the authors have pointed out problems with families, with contemporary work possibilities, and other artifacts of today's living. It is not our intent to maintain the position that abolition of any of these institutions will solve the problems of the human race. We do see their effect, however, and urge the exploration of additional alternatives. Given the problems inherent in families, why do communes, communal marriages, and other alternatives cause such intense reactions in American people? Given that working in a factory is alienating and that being involved in management increases your chances of ulcers and coronary thrombosis, why do parents define themselves and their children as failures, if those children choose not to work in the competitive rat-race? Given the intrinsic conflict present between men and women because of the socialized sex roles of both, why must love relationships between members of the same sex be unlawful and scorned? These authors define contemporary society as producing alienation and conformity among its people. We believe that everyone is taught to believe that identification with a group is essential at all costs. We maintain that those who cannot or do not conform are acting out their frustration in a way which has meaning and intelligibility.

Symptomatology

The third general area to be considered is the theoretical assertions which surround symptoms: how they are used and abused by individuals and the culture. The "nature of symptoms" has long been a battle ground between different theoretical camps.

Comparative Views of Symptomatology

The behaviorists maintain (and have demonstrated with some success) that treating the symptom successfully removes the problem, and the only issue at hand is the most efficient way for the client to learn to live more successfully in his/her environment. Freudian psychology maintains however, that treating the manifest behaviors will only cause the person to exhibit a different maladaptive behavior, because the problem will still exist and has not been affected by treatment of the symptom.

Szasz (1970) posited the first break from either of these two major constructs by calling any difficulty a "problem in living." He advocates the position that problems actually stem from societal causes, and communities at large use the label of pathology as a way of not dealing with the context of the behavior. In that respect the labelling of mental illness is hardly different from the witch hunts of previous times. Szasz goes on to say that mental illness is a myth, that is, it is not true that life will be harmonious if disruptive forces (persons) are removed. There are basic social, ethical, and personal conflicts which are inherent in living, and these are not going to be alleviated by attempting to label, put away, or otherwise invalidate those who do not meet the moral and ethical norms of the community.

The label of "sick" is relatively new to western cultures — replacing concepts such as witches, demons, and other supernaturally-caused deviant behaviors. Along with the "sick" label came the attempt to make mental illness as guilt-free as any other illness. People are not individually blamed for having physical ailments. In recent years television commercials have even been used to proclaim the similarities between mental and physical illness. Everyone was encouraged to think of problems in dealing with one's environment as equal, though dissimilar, to having polio or heart trouble. The effort to remove guilt and shame from our personal problems has been at least partially successful. Movie stars freely discuss their "analyses" on talk shows; encounter groups and gestalt psychology have become the "in" thing to do in some locales.

Social Change Counseling looks at symptoms in a different way. First, within an individual's social context a "symptom" could be a healthy response. It is a survival response, an attempt to manipulate one's environment in order to make it more livable and tolerable. Most people seem to have very "normal" ways of adjusting and changing their immediate environment, but it is possible that a response which appears symptomatic may be the only behavior which is known to be available, or possible, for a particular person to use. Secondly, it is also possible that going to a hospital in the role of a crazy person may seem to be the only means available for some people to deal with their crazy world. In that respect we must say that some symptoms are adaptive.

Laing takes this reasoning one step further and asks what is wrong with a behavior which is a successful attempt NOT to adapt? That is, why is adapting to the culture so valued? If the study of psychology is truly valueless, then the statements "successful adaptation to the culture." and "successful nonadaptation to the culture" should be equally possible outcomes of therapy or of a person's life situation.

Symptoms: A Definition

First, what is a symptom? F. C. Redlich and D. X. Freedman (1969) wrote that behavior which reveals anxiety, depression, confusion, or anger, the cause of which is not apparent to the person experiencing it or those around him/her, is a symptom. This can take on every-day kinds of meanings. When a child is fussy it can be a symptom that he/she does not want to play with other children. When a person is overly sharp with a spouse or neighbor it can be a symptom of a bad night's sleep or some undiscernible physical discomfort. However, if we extend the same principle over longer time periods, it takes on a different character.

For example, the behavior of a teenager who is truant, uses drugs, or does any number of illegal or immoral acts is rarely seen as symptomatic of schools that are uninteresting, of a homelife that is too restrictive, or a society in which he/she finds no meaning. A man or a woman may be impotent or frigid but this is not often attributed to an environment in which they are unloved, a homelife in which they are powerless, or a world which offers them no hope. A person labeled as schizophrenic is not given the alternative of saying the environment produces mixed messages and double-bind situations. When behaviors become relatively permanent adaptations or responses to the environment, those symptoms or behaviors come to be labeled serious, ill or maladaptive, and consequently require attention by others.

Etiology of Symptoms

Secondly, what are the possible meanings of symptoms? A symptom can result from too much stress. The cause of that stress may be internal or external. In this context, symptoms become adaptive and protect the individual from receiving and processing too much data which is emotionally or psychologically burdensome. As such, symptomatic behavior is a statement to the community that this person is under duress. In such situations the person needs to be allowed to express the symptom or to leave or change the circumstances which are causing the stress.

A symptom can also be a means of influencing one's environment. It may be a last ditch effort after having tried more acceptable modes of intervention, or it may be the most plausible, possible, or acceptable interruption of the current succession of events.

Whether the symptom is the result of too much stress or an attempt to influence the environment, it indicates a communication intended to elicit a reaction which will cause change. It is an indirect attempt to influence an environment, which is apparently perceived as incapable of being influenced directly.

Halleck (1971) suggests that symptoms can become "autonomous," that is, become similar to a bad habit. They may continue to exist after the stimulus has changed, and the perpetuation of the symptoms keeps the person from recognizing that they are no longer needed, that the situations for which they were developed no longer exist. For example, a woman who has been unresponsive in a sexual relationship in which she was unhappy might remain so even after she changes partners, not recognizing the situations as different. A student may remain hostile in school, even though the counselor arranged a change in schedule. At this point, the counselor must make a judgment. Is the symptom perpetuating itself, or has the environment not actually changed? Is the woman or the student being treated by others in ways which may be somewhat different but are in essence the same? The therapist must help the client discriminate if the situation is essentially different, and then work on alleviation of the symptom. This points out one of the ways political and moral values operate within a counselor's realm. The decision to work on the symptom because it has become autonomous, or the decision to change the environment is a choice which reflects the political and moral values of the counselor.

Practicing Symptom Psychology

When this discussion of symptoms was undertaken, it was agreed that most of the clients who are seen by professional counselors and therapists would choose adjustment to the culture. When the client presents a symptom, and a goal of therapy is decided mutually, the counselor holds the responsibility for pointing out alternatives which differ from the client's present perspective. A sixteen-year-old woman who wants to get married to a seventeen-year-old man because she is pregnant will usually receive counsel that other alternatives exist even though her original perceptions of the situation may have indicated that no other alternative would be possible for the couple or their respective families. Many counselors now hold the value that other alternatives exist and are able to present those alternatives to the parties involved. Unwanted pregnancies have become a counseling issue which now has more alternatives open than in the past.

When this philosophy is applied to situations upon which there is not as much agreement, situations in which there is less congruence about the acceptable outcomes, it appears that counselors decide they cannot and do not influence their clients' choices. For example, a couple who are seeking relationship counseling may find few counselors who are open to the exploration of their problems if the couple are of the same sex. Likewise a group of persons who all love each other will be hard pressed to find a counselor who will suggest the alternative that they consider group marriage and multiple cohabitation. It seems that a counselor's bag of tricks and lists of alternatives are limited to his/her moral values, usually reflecting middle-class ethics and normality options. It is precisely this activity which substantiates the assertion that therapy, as it is usually practiced, most often offers only adjustment.

If symptom psychology is practiced without also inducing awareness of the societal genesis of the condition, it is potentially repressive. This holds true equally for behaviorists who focus attention on the behavior of the individual and for humanists who focus on what the individual is feeling. Both disregard the role of the environment in producing the feelings and/or the behavior. All the attention is usually focused on helping the client to get along better in the world as it currently exists. (There are a few notable exceptions among the behaviorists, primarily the recent interest in assertive training, and those who base much of their plans for change on environmental manipulation.) The argument that the counselor only has the right/obligation to teach those behaviors or influence those feelings which the client presents as problematic is often used as a cop-out. This provides a reasonable rationale for not exploring areas of the client's world which are potentially explosive and political in nature. This argument is quickly forgotten, however, when the counselor decides that there is something the client needs "to explore."

Symptoms in a Cultural Context

Thus far we have been looking at symptoms essentially from the vantage point of the individual and, to some extent, from the angle of the therapist. In this approach it is also essential to consider the cultural role in the labeling and use of symptoms. Because what is considered symptomatic of an internal problem varies considerably from culture to culture, we must conclude that symptoms are, to a large degree, culturally bound and culturally defined. For example, aggression would be indicative of a personal problem if found within an American Indian tribe whereas passivity is more likely diagnosed as symptomatic for contemporary white boys. Likewise, in this society, the behavior of female children is expected to lie at the passive end of the active-passive continuum. In matriarchal societies the reverse is true.

Although the issue will be further developed when considering deviance, it is pertinent at this point to ask what a society gains by labeling its deviants as defective. Perhaps a look at the consequence of that activity will provide a clue. First and foremost, labeling any problem as a personal problem (whether it is done in behavioristic or psychoanalytic terminology) tends to remove the responsibility from the environment which was the cause of the behavior. This shift in emphasis takes the pressure off, refocuses the attention, and decreases the possibility that the culture might be found at fault.

Secondly, the identification of the person as having a problem invalidates what the person might say. An inmate of a psychiatric hospital could not possibly talk about inhumane conditions present there — after all, he/she is paranoid schizophrenic. Similarly, a juvenile labeled "delinquent" commands no attention when speaking of life in a poor neighborhood or of the problems with irrelevant schooling. This invalidation is perhaps the most serious crime our society commits. The critics, the ones who perceive it as a problem to live the way they are living, are rendered illegitimate and inappropriate.

Finally, by the use of symptoms — in this sense the "psychiatric excuse" — it is possible to alleviate one's responsibilities. This can happen in two ways. First, the sick role allows a person extra benefits, special considerations, and at least an exemption from guilt should he/she fail. Knowing the assured result of developing symptoms, one can very adaptively escape problems and responsibilities almost at will. Secondly, the power of the psychiatric excuse can remove one from unpleasant situations, if one has the money, influence, or position to obtain that excuse. That is, psychiatric excuses for abortions, exemptions from the draft, annulment of marriages, changing class schedules, altering college living arrangements, and a host of other situations are possible with a needed psychiatric signature. In fact, it is often thought by professionals to be the humane, even liberal, thing to do to grant such excuses, perhaps as an attempt to fight back in one small way. The effect, however, has been somewhat different. In the larger picture it is possible to predict that abortion on demand, the removal of the draft, and improvement in college dormitories and other humane activities might have happened sooner if those who protested had not been exempted and quit their battle. Halleck (1971) points out just such an occurrence at the University of Wisconsin. Following his refusal, as chief of the psychiatric services, to give permission for persons to be excused from living in university housing on psychiatric grounds, those persons who had requested such exceptions worked within the dormitory system to improve living conditions. Dormitories were then more tolerable for a larger percentage of students. Although this may have truly placed a burden upon those who lived there before the changes were made, it provided benefits to many who would never have received the excuse.

Although this discussion of symptoms has been approached from many angles, essentially it has attempted to explain that symptoms are not the result of a personal malfunction; they result from environmental causes (excluding those which are organic). Therefore, the focus on a person's symptoms reinforces the notion that problems are inherent within the person and not arising from the milieu. Symptoms allow the culture to escape responsibility for its actions and invalidate the criticism lodged by deviant persons. It is maintained that counselors have a responsibility to their clients to share what awareness they have achieved about possible causes of those symptomatic behaviors.

Deviance

At first glance, it is confusing to think of separating symptomotology and deviance. Although there is certainly an overlap in many cases, the authors take the position that deviance is a variation from the cultural norm or subgroup, or an expressed difference from those around you. This is distinguished from those whose personal adaptation to the world is in some manner personally unique. Perhaps it is clearest to say that you are a deviant if you fit into a defined group — campus rebel, homosexual, anarchist — about which there is some established, labeled identification. Although these groups are often labeled as exhibiting behavior which is symptomatic of personal problems, they usually find their deviation a difficulty only because others are not comfortable with their values or life styles. In this discussion of deviance, we will include a definition, the etiology, some of the effects of the label "deviant," its historical justification and use as a scapegoat.

Deviance: A Definition

It is interesting to reflect upon what type of deviations are considered ethically good and which ones are problems. A case could be made for the notion that celibacy in priests and nuns is deviant and indicative of a problem which needs societal attention. Consider also the deviation of expansive power wishes which are manifested "legitimately" by most politicians. A research scientist who forsakes all personal and social encounters in hopes of a breakthrough in his/her work certainly does deviate from the normal population. These deviations, however, are lauded as acceptable, perhaps even commendatory. Our acceptance of individual differences does not stretch to include welfare mothers with large families or those who see violence as the only route toward societal change.

Because of a rather tenuous fishnet of acceptable behaviors and life styles, a definition of what is deviant is illusive. Essentially, it includes those who are not average, normal, or similar to everyone else, unless the particular differences in some way earn hero or heroine status. Even though the motives, activities, or consequences may be equally adaptive or nonadaptive to a particular person's situation, one is labeled a hero/heroine if the culture decides to applaud him/her, and a deviant if it does not approve. As before, the question arises as to why the culture needs such strict definitions of that which is acceptable.

Because psychiatrists, in recent decades, began the attempts to formalize what was normal, and because of their power to make that definition, abnormality has come to be viewed as sick. Halleck traces the progression in this manner: those who behave differently are eventually clients of a professional. It is unknown if they behave differently because they are unhappy or if society's restrictions on their behavior makes them unhappy. Whichever it is, the correlation exists between being different and being unhappy. This results in psychologists treating people who are both unhappy and different. "Because he views his patient's unhappiness as a form of illness, he eventually learns to think of his patient's 'difference' as a manifestation of illness [Halleck, 1971, p. 112]."

Etiology of Deviance

Consider the manner and means by which some members choose, are forced to accept, or are socialized to be deviant. Honigman (1967) explains that a person's personality is the result of individual potential in interaction with the environment's expectations. In deviant personalities, the person has accentuated the individual aspect and de-emphasized the cultural expectations. He goes on to add that deviants have failed to internalize the social norms because: 1) the environmental conditions prevented him/her from receiving them; 2) the norms were not comprehended; or 3) the person rebelled and withdrew endorsement of the norms.

Others have added 4) modeling of deviant norms, 5) a reaction to stress (perhaps more closely associated with symptoms but not exclusively), and 6) the process of being labeled deviant. These factors will be elaborated upon briefly.

First, isolation from the cultural mainstream is an obvious example of failing to receive the social norms. This could be fostered by exclusive contact with an ethnic subgroup which had not incorporated certain values. Second, norms might not be comprehended because other opposing values had been learned or the foundations of the norms had not been properly inculcated. Third, development of a political, philosophical, or moral commitment which was contrary to the mainstream values can produce a rejection of previous instruction. Fourth, the behaviors and attitudes of someone who appears to a youngster to have "it made" by deviating from the rules better than those who follow the rules will present a strong stimulus to model those behaviors so that similar benefits will be attained. It is of little surprise that drug addiction and crime are more related to neighborhoods than to personality type. Fifth, as was noted before, the human animal has seemingly innate capacities for self-protection. If the equilibrium of the individual is threatened, some new behavior will emerge as a safety valve. The role of labeling in the etiology of deviance will be considered in the next section.

Effects of Labeling

Last, the act of labeling someone as deviant plays a major role in contributing to that delinquency. It has been documented extensively by H. S. S. Becker in *Outsiders* (1963) that the crucial step in building a stable deviant career comes with publicly labeling a person a trouble maker, a failure, a drug addict, a homosexual, a delinquent or any other type of deviant. At that point, if the person accepts the label, then the prophecy will be fulfilled.

Honigman (1967) asserts that the degree to which a person identifies, either consciously or unconsciously, with other individuals, with a group, or with a social category will determine the extent to which he/she will move to compliance or noncompliance with that individual, group or category. If that is true, it is easy to see how some ethnic groups, religious sects, women, and other oppressed groups will continue to believe values which are outside the normal structure.

It is somewhat ironic that even deviance is not original. The effect of the culture, its patterning, is found in the manner and mode in which some members choose to be different. Although modeling contributes to this phenomenon, essentially all new acts are variations on the themes already tried by thousands and are ways which the culture has allowed, and perhaps even structured, its loopholes. The types of deviance persons use seem to have a direct correlation with economic and social class. Middle-class norms dictate cheating on income tax or school exams, reckless driving, and premarital sex as close to the norm but slightly unacceptable. Lower class deviance might include common-law marriages, unemployment, and dropping out of school or repeating grades.

In examining the effects of deviant role-playing and labeling, it is important to consider the individual involved and the culture which issues the label. First, the individual might be allowed to escape a situation in society which is less than ideal by playing a deviant role. He/she is provided with a "psychiatric excuse" to make an escape. Conjecture suggests that because of such a situation, a person might learn to manipulate indirectly the environment — as opposed to confronting it — in order to gain what is essentially justified. A more serious issue, however, comes from the self-fulfilling nature of the labeling. Is it possible to be a drug addict, an atheist, a homosexual, or a John Bircher (or any other group which has grown significant enough to have earned a label), at one time and then decide that your values have changed? Rarely does this occur, for it seems that deviant careers become stable because the label never really leaves. As recommendations from past jobs, data banks about personal and social matters become the norm, it will grow increasingly difficult for a person to leave the past behind and start anew.

Halleck (1971), in reference to the individual effects of such labeling, asserted that many persons suffer deeply as a result of being defined as abnormal. Further, even if the psychiatrist does not label individual people, the therapist's attitudes and public pronouncements can contribute to keeping in a state of subjugation deviant individuals and groups who are already oppressed.

An unfortunate and mysterious by-product of being within a labeled deviant group, almost irrespective of the group, is the assumption that deviants cannot control themselves. Perhaps this can be traced to the Freudian theory in which the goal of all persons is the sublimation of the evil, pleasurable forces which are constantly welling within. Perhaps it is a throwback to the idea of daimonic possession; that a disturbed person could never be responsible because it was impossible to predict when the demon might take charge. Whatever the beginning, it has no basis in fact. A person who is an imprudent and obnoxious drunk is deemed capable of self control. When the label alcoholic is attached, the person is no longer thought to possess self-control and loses the rights and privileges of one who is thought more capable. A middle-aged man who is sexually involved with a teenage girl might be thought gross, insensitive, or stupid, however, if he is called a pedophiliac his rationality and capacity for self-control are assumed nonexistent (Halleck, 1971). There is no research or clinical evidence which substantiates the myths of uncontrollability.

The effect on the culture is more subtle, but many, including Erich Fromm, have warned about the price of setting our standards of normality. First, as has been developed throughout this monograph, the focus of problems as personal, and the act of invalidating someone who is different have political consequences, essentially the reinforcement of the status quo. Secondly, whenever any group is lost from total productivity within the culture, there is loss by the group at large. Personal difficulties resulting from labeling might well have cost the world a scientist, or a poet, or, at least, a person who was happy. It is hard to think that we can afford the cost of either. Unfortunately, the label of deviant justifies ignoring a person.

Because deviance is identified in this way, society is given permission to treat certain persons or groups as second-class citizens. Although true stonings (as were common in Biblical times for those who had violated the mores) are seldom experienced in this century, job discrimination, public ridicule, and inhumane living conditions are not uncommon. This permission explains the vast discrepancies between the professed Judeo-Christian-humanistic ethics of western cultures and the realities that exist for many people. It initiates some of the disillusionment in youth who have become aware of those variances.

The Historical Perspective

Historical investigation gives us precedents for many of the current myths about oppressed groups. All nonreproductive sex was outlawed during the Middle Ages because it was important to increase the labor force. During the 1800's in America, when many persons were needed to populate the West, similar laws were enacted in the United States. Those laws were rational and understandable for those periods of time. They do not make sense today. Similarly, laws relating to women were instituted at a time when it was important for all members of the family to be at home and share in the rearing of children and cultivating of the land. This also is not required with the advent of modern appliances, fewer children, increased education for women, and the need of our nation for all available person power. Similar parallels can be found for children and racial and ethnic groups.

It is equally understandable that those in power, whether the system is large or small, will continue to perpetuate those myths so that the oppression appears justified. Psychology has used its power to reinforce many of those myths and has deterred society from confronting its inequities. Because oppressed groups will continue in their state of subjugation until they feel it is inappropriate, broad socialization about inferiority and superiority seeks to maintain the present power balance.

Deviance in a Cultural Context

Our last topic concerning deviance investigates the question which has been asked throughout the preceding pages: why does society seem to demand that a deviant label, scorn, and oppression be heaped upon those who do not conform? The answer which is used by those who do the labeling and the scorning is that there is something wrong with those people who are abnormal, and the rest of society must be protected from them. It appears the deviants' ideas and influence are feared by those in power.

First, the concept of deviance is used as a scapegoat to account for problems and provide a reason for the world not running smoothly. Szasz (1970) asserts that there is an illusion that problems will not arise in the daily course of living. He states that the only way we can ever stop our search for the reasons why life does not progress perfectly is to accept the reality that it never will. American idealism, which supports the belief in perfect love, families without trauma, and interpersonal relationships without disagreements and conflict, must be confronted.

Secondly, for some, deviance provides a personal excuse. It may be a parent who wants to alleviate any potential guilt for an offspring's difficulties in life, or a person who would like to slip in under the umbrella of having problems so that past or present slights or mistakes might be overlooked. Primarily, the use of deviance as a personal excuse seems to stem from a lack of awareness. Most Americans have not been taught to analyze, criticize, and plan alternatives to their social systems. Many find it beyond comprehension to imagine a socialization that is different. The "us-them" orientation has been ingrained so deeply that it is impossible to consider crossing over the boundary line to the other side.

Lastly, society uses the deviant label out of fear. For example, the loudest female opponents of the Equal Rights Amendment are often afraid to examine what they might be able to do if they were not staying at home; the person who protests the most about effeminate men is likely to have concerns about his own virility. Otherwise, why would it matter? It is the opinion of the authors that all the above reasons are defensive: they are explaining away a phenomenon that seems otherwise inexplicable, that otherwise might push for a personal confrontation.

Summary

It is perhaps difficult to discern components of the theory of Social Change Counseling from the preceding discourse. That responsibility is accepted by the authors but shared with the newness of this approach. In an attempt to consolidate what has been said, the following brief summary is included.

The nature of persons includes a political attribute which is probably learned. People's free will has been conditioned away from them partially by the desire to have the approval of others. Intimacy is important, but there are strict rules about when and how it is appropriate. Change is inherent but people have limits concerning the amount they can experience. Most people look for some explanation of their existence and its meaning.

Many Americans are apathetic and unable to think critically about their existence. Living in families contributes to learning powerlessness, interdependency, and the "us-them" dichotomy. These are reflected in adults who are, as a rule, anxious and alienated.

Symptoms have a social intelligibility and may constitute a healthy response to the environment. They are often initiated as an attempt to influence the environment and are, at least, a statement about its present condition. The focus on symptoms in treatment reinforces the erroneous belief that problems are a result of a personal malfunction and not a consequence of the culture. The labeling of the person as having the problem further invalidates his/her own critique and criticisms and provides many with a psychiatric excuse. Both of these deter the goals of social change.

Deviance results from impaired socialization for one or more of many possible reasons. The use of deviance as a label is the tool of the culture to influence groups and masses of people. Although many of the myths about deviant or oppressed groups have foundations in history, they are no longer appropriate even as defenses.

3

Techniques

How does one evolve technique from theory? How does one concretize a philosophical orientation into an active approach? It is possible to extend theory in many and varied directions, but that theory is useless unless it can be tested in practice. The proponents of the Social Change approach to counseling are at this juncture of attempting to make practical application of a theory and a philosophy. Some inroads have been made by trying out applications. Much has been learned from the work of social workers, radical therapists, and counselors interested in implementing social change. However, since the Social Change approach is in its formative stages, it is continuing to look for new and unique ways to make practical application of the theory. A basic direction has been taken, what remains is a rounding out, extension, and refinement of procedures. Because much is still founded in formulation and speculation, this chapter may be frustrating to those who are looking for a step-by-step presentation of how to be a society-based counselor. (The next chapter containing case illustrations may be helpful to some.) What will be offered is the knowledge gained from the experience of those who are striving to implement this type of theory. At other points it must suffice to relate only conjecture of what applications could be made from the theory.

For some, being part of the therapeutic establishment is a great moral and philosophical dilemma. Acting as a therapist and implementing social change may well be a contradiction in terms. Many of the radical will agree that there are people who have great skill and facility in talking with and helping others, that some seem to be more sensitive human beings than others. These individuals with such skills may not be and very often are not professionally trained. The radical will also agree that, for some individuals, a refuge from the pressures of day-to-day living may be necessary and that medication may be useful for others. However, it is the opinion of many, including the authors, that such departures should be brief and always as preparation for a return to society. These interventions do not have to be occasions of oppression.

The authors feel that counselors can only justify their professional existence by using their skills to help their clients explore to the fullest all the possible alternatives that could be available to them in their situations. Counselors have an obligation to confront the status quo and not to preach and reinforce sameness or adjustment. As change agents, counselors have the moral responsibility to take issue with the social order, to look for new and varied alternatives. Changing behavior in the direction of conformity or voluntary (or involuntary) commitment could take away one more person who might have contributed to social change. Counselors who use their skills in these ways are making a political statement and are retarding progress toward a society which will respond to the needs of all its members. Very often those who find fault with society as it is presently functioning or who develop symptoms resulting from societal stress are labeled as deviants. This labeling is often done by members of the therapeutic profession and then echoed by others who are in contact with those labeled "deviants." They are now "second-class citizens" and any attempt which they might make to change those systems which are causing problems will be invalidated because they have been instigated by those of "deviant" status. Attacks on oppressive practices are scoffed at if they are made by someone who has or has had "emotional problems." Why is it inappropriate for the victims of society's mistreatment and disregard to raise their voices in protest? These types of protest are somehow not legitimate, and every time a counselor labels, institutionalizes, or "cools off" such a victim, one potential voice has been quieted, his/her potential or past protest invalidated, and we are one step farther removed from instituting meaningful social change.

This chapter will present ways in which those in the helping professions can avoid these outcomes. In order to do so, the presentation will deal with three different areas: self-reform or consciousness raising for therapists; techniques to influence large social systems, and finally, techniques to influence small social systems (e.g., families, peer groups).

Therapist Self-Reform or Consciousness Changing

Regarding the area of self-reform, it is the conviction of the authors that Social Change Counseling cannot be practiced by those who have little political awareness, who ignore social issues, or who prefer to "stick their heads in the sand" rather than confront the moral dilemmas of modern society. One cannot relate individual problems to political or social causes if he/she has no idea of the possible systems or practices which could potentially contribute to an individual's distress. One cannot make inferences or political analyses without some knowledge of the operations of political and social systems and the uses and abuses of power. Because every encounter with a client has political implications, all who work in the helping professions have an obligation to explore the possible implications and long-range effects of their work.

An initial step in enhancing political and social awareness is to undertake a careful self-examination. Look at your career choice in the light of wanting to help people even though you are oppressing them for the system. In terms of your own practices, the contradiction may manifest itself in your belief that you are acting as a "helper" to the client when the long-range effect of this work is to bolster the status quo and reinforce conformity. There is a further contradiction that warrants scrutiny: that of wanting to help people while making a living from their suffering. Without a clientele the economic status and professional prowess of the therapist would wither. Many therapists contend that they would like to be "put out of business" and see an end to emotional trauma, but they have an economic investment in the problems of others. In examining your own orientation to the profession these are important issues to resolve.

An additional area which warrants confrontation is personal rigidity. This may be seen as identification with the system, with a certain social class and the privileges that it engenders. Counselors are members of an intellectual elite and certain privileges occur naturally from this position of power, e.g., borrowing money, enhanced mobility, the luxury and security of a family physician, interesting leisure pastimes, and the accumulation of wealth and possessions. These privileges frequently separate members of the helping profession from their clientele making it difficult for either to identify with the other. It is especially the "underprivileged" who feel this difference and rely significantly less on counselors or therapists to help them with troubling situations. Confronting personal rigidity may lead to working through elitist attitudes by identifying those groups you openly or covertly list as "second-class citizens." This will then require structured consciousness-changing experiences.

As counselors and therapists most of us like to think of ourselves as unbiased, with unconditional positive regard (or at least positive regard) for all individuals, regardless of their backgrounds or stations in life. However, a more reasonable assumption under which to operate is that, as members of the white middle class (which most people in the therapeutic professions are), we have learned certain biases as a result of our socialization process. Operating under this assumption is more realistic than the assumption that we are bias-free or culture-fair. Taking for granted that our awareness can be heightened and that we can learn to be less prejudiced will open one to enlightening educational experiences and to the opportunity of making changes in attitudes and behavior.

If additional help in recognizing areas for self-improvement is needed, seek out members of minority groups (e.g., feminists, homosexuals, individuals of differing racial and ethnic origins) and ask them to listen to your opinions, or to critique a tape recording of a counseling interview to point out biased statements or condescending interactions. These individuals can inform you of topics or word usages that are particularly sensitive to them and ways in which they would prefer to be considered. For example, you can shake up sexism in your own written and spoken language by using he/she for the impersonal third person. The reliance on the use of the masculine pronoun when gender is unknown is both inaccurate and offensive.

Other methods of stimulating social and political consciousness include reading literature of groups whose views are in opposition to yours. This is designed to provoke thought, discussion, and understanding and cause a questioning of personal views. Attending minority groups' educational and informational sessions can influence your self-examination. The formation of consciousness-changing groups is a good tool in confronting your rigidity with the support and help of the group members.

Increased political and social awareness can be developed by the exploration of alternative life styles and institutions either for the purposes of increasing your own awareness of less conventional life-options, choosing an alternative life style or career, or presenting such a choice to your clients. Day care co-ops, food co-ops, communal living, and Vocations for Social Change emphasize living collectively, sharing skills and self-sufficiency. Though not without problems of their own, these options are attracting increasing numbers of people who are dissatisfied with society as it is now structured, traditional relationships, and repressive or undesirable careers.

The aforementioned attempts at self-reform have mainly been in the personal realm, to help you as a human being expand your choices of action and thinking. What follows will focus on you as a professional "helper." We will paraphrase the suggestion made earlier. Make the assumption that, no matter how careful you feel you have been, you have engaged in repressive therapeutic practices, you have not explored all possible alternative courses of action with your clients, and you have taught clients to adjust to a world which needs changing. In order to modify your way of analyzing client situations, you will need practice drawing new and different conclusions (and in sharing these with your clients). Begin by examining the ways political and social institutions and practices have influenced your behavior and attitudes and those of your clients. Pay particular attention to the stresses which they engender. Look at how power and privilege are exercised to oppress certain types of individuals and groups. When scrutinizing radical movements, analyze them not in a psychodynamic way, but as responses to political and social stresses. The latter analysis will have more validity and meaning for clients than the former.

In continuing this kind of self-education, attempt to find correlates of the concepts that were presented in the first chapter. This can be done by analyzing situations using the theories of Merton, Laing, Scheff, Szasz, Halleck, and the Radical Therapists. Of course this re-education process takes time, practice, and commitment, but may be aided by assembling a group of like-minded colleagues who are equally interested in seeking out alternatives to traditional therapeutic approaches. Together you can read, share information and analyses, and try out new techniques. If these colleagues are employed by the same institution, include in the focus of the group an examination of that institution's practices, with an eye toward changing repressive practices. The adage, "Physician, heal thyself [and thy surroundings]" is appropriately mentioned at this juncture. While taking to task your practices and those of the institution which employs you, also confront reactionary professional notions concerning sex, race, sexual preference, and criminal behavior. (The reader is referred to the sections on deviance and symptomatology in Chapter 2.)

Halleck (1971) presents some salient issues regarding professional practices of counselors and therapists. He suggests severely restricting the use of psychological tests, because they are more often than not used to grant or deny privileges. (The authors would also include intelligence testing in this restricted classification.) He further asserts that by granting psychiatric excuses for responsibilities (e.g., military service, abortion), the practitioner is offering yet another privilege to the social elite (who can afford such consultation) and is contributing to the preservation of the status quo. His/her efforts would be better spent in trying to reform these practices. It is also the duty of the professional to stop the perpetuation of myths which contribute to the oppression of blacks, women, and other groups. In addition, the therapist should not honor requests by government agencies or insurance companies to provide information about former clients. Perhaps, the most important issue is the need to stop the use of psychiatric diagnostic labels and to consider the social consequences which this labeling process has for clients. To further encourage the demise of labeling, it is possible to make public the arbitrariness of this categorization which only lends to the myths surrounding the profession. To end this section on self-reform we will again quote from Halleck.

> Psychiatrists [and other mental health professionals] must immediately stop all propaganda designed to convince the public that mental illness is a disease just like any other disease. Instead, they should publicly acknowledge that some behavior disorders resemble physical illness and others do not. They should explain the advantages and disadvantages of the mental illness role and they should tell the public whatever they know about the causes of human suffering [1971, p. 313].

Change In Large Social Systems

What has been said up to this point concerning technique and that which is to follow greatly emphasize the counselor's or therapist's role in actively working toward social change. The activist counselor cannot sit back and wait for others to take up the gauntlet or expect that only the effected clients have a responsibility to press for the change of oppressive conditions. Certainly the counselor cannot actively participate in every struggle for reform. As human beings we have been endowed with neither infinite energy nor resources. However, it is possible to lend personal support in varying degrees to different groups or movements which enhance people's political consciousness. Once you have come to an understanding of the alternatives to which you wish to devote the greatest amount of time and energy, it is incumbent on you to take a stand and to take a positive action in becoming an involved member.

The authors will present first the means of effecting changes in large social systems such as schools or hospitals. Later we will focus on working with clients or client groups to effect large social systems. Some of the suggestions which may be useful in your attempts at change will also be valuable as suggestions which you can give to your clients.

Because an ordered sequence of events which will effect social change is not known at this time, the suggestions given will not follow any specific order. Where one step would seem logically to precede another, this information will be included. The majority of the tactics which are proposed for changing large social systems are public in nature, i.e., geared to be seen and reacted to, to be felt by more than one person, and to start people thinking. Glenn and Kunnes (1973) remark that the main task of therapists should not be to preserve their skills but to change their life situation. Concretely, therapists are encouraged to integrate themselves with different segments of the population, especially those who do not enjoy similar middle- and upper-class privileges, to reduce the gap between therapist and potential clients.

Professionals need to be involved in the community as active "regular" persons to experience the struggles of causing change, to help demystify "the profession," and to add strength to the movement. One main theme of several authors is the need for decentralization of power. Many large (and small) social institutions are failing to respond to the needs of the people that they are supposed to serve. Members of a community can join together to seek control of the institutions within their communities. Students have and will continue to press for more meaningful input into the policies of their schools. Community members can insist on playing a role in the selection of mental health professionals who work at their local mental health centers. Community members can best identify the needs of their own community and should have a responsibility in trying to meet those needs. Selection of mental health workers who can offer the most beneficial services in ways which the community finds acceptable is one way to implement that responsibility. Further, increased community involvement in social institutions will aid in the demystification of these institutions, their inner workings no longer secretive and their professionals no longer encased in ivory towers. It can well be your task as a therapist/counselor to help organize such a community group and to be part of such a group in your own community. The institutions into which you seek input are not limited to the areas of health and education, but could include local, regional, and national government, law enforcement, and environmental and social welfare systems. As many have said, the problems of individuals in our society are too pervasive, too widespread to support the illusion that their causes rest within individuals. Those of us in the mental health professions, who are confronted daily with these problems, must decide whether or not we will start to do something to change the external environment for all those who suffer from it.

An important point to be considered, whether encouraging community involvement in social action or participating in that action as a member of the community, concerns the establishment of alternative centers or institutions. It is the opinion of some, including the authors, that the establishment of alternative service centers (e.g., drug "crash" centers, community medical services) or the provision of the psychiatric excuse, relieves the obligation of established institutions to deal with socially-caused problems. In a social system that is imposing massive oppression upon large numbers of its members, efforts to gain preferential treatment for a few will further regard the slow process of change. It is more likely that institutions and systems will change, or will be forced to change, when their glaring inadequacies are exposed, when people are in need but can find no assistance. Such inadequacies are rarely exposed when an alternative center or service has been set up to meet unmet needs. Only infrequently does the public make the connection that because an alternative center has been established, there must be a fault in some institution which needs to be corrected. Even less frequently will the public go on to press for steps to correct that fault.

A dilemma may result from not giving preferential treatment to a needy few. Failing to offer immediate assistance to some in lieu of long-range changes in the environment may involve too great a sacrifice. One possible resolution of this conflict is the establishment of alternative centers as a short-range solution to the problem with the ultimate goal being to change the institution or system to respond (or respond more satisfactorily) to that problem. This sort of approach would consider the organization of alternative centers as only secondary, with the awareness that it would be self-defeating to consider the work done when the center was begun. The final goal of changing the institution must never be out of sight, lest it be forgotten. Should the establishment of a center or service be the final outcome of a social action project, then the more meaningful long-range goal has been sacrificed, the environment will not be changed for the many who suffer from it. An example of one group who kept their sights focused on a long-range goal concerns a cluster of community members who were working for a change in the public school system to make it responsive to the needs of all of its students (i.e., non-college bound, culturally different). This group did start an alternative school, but realized that this school could serve only limited numbers of students, from limited areas of the city. They also realized that ultimately the responsibility for serving these students rested with the public school system. They continued to press for change within the schools, and eventually change was accomplished for the benefit of many students.

Another area in which counselors or therapists can work to bring about change is their work environment. It is possible to see this environment as a community in which active participation by its members is sought and needed. As a member of such a "work community," your efforts can be best directed at making the institution responsive to the needs of its "work community" and its geographic community. One way to accomplish this is to expose the deficiencies of the institution and urge a change in services. Most institutions could be more responsive to community needs if they developed innovative services. These innovative services might well include preventative attention rather than the usual, too-late attempts at remediation. As a staff member, the counselor or therapist wields much power in bringing about such changes. As stated previously, in working toward self-reform, practitioners can organize self-help discussion groups to work toward this end. These groups can also direct their energies toward pressing for institutional changes. After all, the ultimate goal of the re-educative self-reform process is to put these new ideas into action by carrying out a plan to implement social change. Different groups can be formed to reflect individuals' differing states of political awareness. Some may prefer consciousness-changing groups, while others would opt for a radical study caucus.

A further way in which the therapist or counselor can bring the Social Change approach to the attention of co-workers is by presenting client case histories at staff conferences, emphasizing politically relevant points. In addition, concerned staff and residents of an institution can work together in putting out a newsletter directed at pointing out the needs of its work and resident communities and pushing for responsiveness and responsibility on the part of the institution.

Having reached a midpoint in this discussion of effecting change in large social systems, it now seems relevant to make reference to information and suggestions that will be useful both to you and your clients in implementing change strategies. Social work literature provides a basis from which to start, especially the approach of Ellen Manser in *Family Advocacy, A Manual For Action* (1973), which is cited in part below. Though written as a guideline for family advocacy, her system can be used for many other types of change projects.

1. Know your case. Identify the problem and its probable cause.
2. "Know both sides of the case." Identify the sources of conflict and the opinions of the opposition.
3. "Learn how the systems work." Know the policies, procedures, goals, and people in power in the institutions that are causing distress.
4. Know available sources of information and use them when needed. Legal or medical advice may be very pertinent.
5. Discover others who may be working on the same problem or issue that you are involved in. If your goals are similar, decide whether your proposed methods are compatible, and if they are, determine how best to combine forces. Some may be more effective as leaders, while others could be background supporters or members of a coalition.
6. "Check your case. Do you have all the information and documentation you need? Do you know your potential allies and potential enemies?" Are you sure of your role in the change process?
7. Make an accurate analysis of the problem and "form an effective treatment plan or strategy for bringing about change. Mobilize allies."
8. Weigh the risks of action versus inactivity. "Plan to protect the most vulnerable (usually the client) from paying too high a price for a small gain."
9. Try to enlist the support of people in high levels of influence and policy making.
10. "Understand that changing an institution is usually a long process involving hard work, persistence, disappointment,

and only occasional moments of high drama or notable success."

11. "Work for cooperation and voluntary change but never refuse to confront if this alternative becomes necessary."
12. "Evaluate progress. If it has been sufficient to achieve the goals, consider the factors that led to success and be generous with credit to all those who contributed, including those in the system who changed. . . . If the problem was not corrected, study the situation again. What information was lacking? What were the unforeseen barriers? What mistakes in strategy were made? Do not close the case but make a new treatment plan based on experience to date."*

Manser also delineates some guidelines related to the evaluation of family advocacy programs which can be applied to other change projects (pp. 58–59):

1. "Is the goal to change a system that is hurting people?"
2. Is the goal assurance of the right of all individuals to services?

In underscoring the need for follow through she points out that:

1. "Change may not become real without monitoring to make sure that those who liked the old way are not still practicing that way even if law or policy has changed."
2. Was the change big enough to accomplish the objective?
3. "Giving people who are being hurt by a system the opportunity to ventilate their feelings or share their concerns is a service, but it is not advocacy [or Social Change Counseling] until the agency [counselor, or action group] provides avenues for changing the offending system." In fact ventilation and sharing of concerns may discourage people from taking social action because it reduces both their anxiety and anger and decreases their motivation to work for change.
4. "Gathering of information is a basic step in advocacy [or Social Change Counseling] but without further activity to resolve the problem thus identified and documented there has been no advocacy service [or movement toward change]."*

At this point the focus of the discussion will shift to techniques for working with individual clients or client groups. Implicit in the

* From Ellen Manser, ed., *Family Advocacy*, pp. 54–56, 58–59, © 1973 by Family Service Association of America. Reprinted by permission.

philosophical position of Social Change Counseling is that the counselor or therapist looks upon the client as an equal. Therefore, no hierarchical system is set up with the client on the bottom rung. To implement this position the counselor or therapist may share his/her feelings when they have been similar to those of the client. This lends support and credibility to thoughts and feelings which the client may have felt made him/her unusual or even "crazy." When the counselor or therapist reveals similar thoughts and concerns, the client experiences some relief in knowing that he/she is not the only one who has ever felt that way. The counselor quite possibly may not have had thoughts or reactions similar to the client's. If not, he/she could relate similar reactions to a different situation or reflect that it is possible to see how the client could be led to certain feelings or actions.

Part of the therapeutic process should include an explanation of how political, social, and economic pressures cause people to feel and act in certain ways. Family or institutional practices may leave individuals feeling alienated from each other, without the ability to exercise choice and free will, exploited by those with money and power, and, though ill at ease with their life situation, reluctant to let this be known lest they be labeled "abnormal." By giving a political analysis of the causes of clients' problems and by teaching this method of analysis, the counselor or therapist makes progress toward lifting a burden from clients who think that their problems are their fault. People feel less "crazy" or less troubled when they come to see that their "troubles have their source not within them but in their alienated relationships, in their exploitation, in polluted environments, in war, and in the profit motive [Steiner, 1971]." When the counselor or therapist confirms the client's reality, or accepts his/her reality as a possibility, the client can feel a sense of community with those who have similar problems. Anger, which had previously been directed inwardly, can now be channeled outward and directed toward causing change.

At this point the client is confronted with three different options which the counselor or therapist can aid in bringing to awareness:

1. Remain in the problem situation, making no changes or adjustments, but with an awareness of the source of the problem.
2. Learn to live with (adjust to) the problem situation. The client changes his/her behavior or thoughts about the problem.
3. Change the environmental stimulus which is the source of

the problem, by acting as a political, social or economic change agent.

If the client should choose to exercise one of the first two options, the social change counselor may be confronted with a conflict in values such that it may be necessary to refer the client to a counselor or therapist who can help carry out those options. The client who makes the choice to work toward changing the environment, however, must know that "his/her capacity to change an oppressive environment depends on psychological strength, awareness of what the environment is doing to him/her, and motivation to change [Halleck, 1971, p. 36]." These variables will have an effect when the client feels prepared to begin change activity. The client must decide whether the oppressive environment is worth changing. If it is, the client may choose to either participate in a radical restructuring of the environment or in a project focused on reform. Once the target of this activity is further defined, the counselor or therapist can assist the client in developing several alternative strategies for implementing change.

At this stage, the counselor may direct the client to journal articles or other written materials (particularly from *Radical Therapist/Rough Times*) which discuss how individuals with similar problems dealt with their situations by social action. This may give the client ideas on how to plan action, benefiting from the experiences of others. From these articles the client may also locate groups of individuals with a similar problem who are organized to combat that problem. Joining such a group would offer the client a support base, the strength of increased numbers, and the possibility of group social action. The counselor or therapist should also be aware of organizations in the community with which the client might join forces, and the alternative institutions or life styles to which the client might turn. These groups might include Women's Liberation, Gay Liberation, Insane Liberation, various worker and trade unions, food and housing cooperatives, groups concerned with the rights of children, local, regional and national political organizations, and other types of groups.

In attempting to bring about change in large social systems, it is very unlikely that one individual working alone will have enough time, energy, knowledge, and influence to implement widespread change. For this reason it is recommended that the client with this purpose in mind either seek out or form a group directed at changing large social systems. As an alternative to seeking out the groups mentioned above, the counselor may assist the client in the formation of a client group. By this is meant any local grouping of individuals who have had contact with the counselor or the agency in which the counselor works and who share a problem. The services of the counselor or therapist may be limited to providing an impetus to the formation of the group. Depending on the wishes of the group, the counselor or therapist may offer further consultation, help the group gain information or access to key individuals, assist in collaborative efforts with other community groups, or aid in the formation of coalitions of groups. The counselor or therapist may utilize his/her skills in assisting the group in role playing proposed actions, in working at problem solving, and by suggesting possible alternatives. The counselor or therapist must guard against being too directive with the group and supporting its dependency upon him/her.

Client groups, or other types of action groups, can engage themselves in a variety of activities directed at social change. Though the specific may be different according to the type of group and the type of change desired, some general activities can be enumerated: 1) educational meetings to alert the public and press to their cause; 2) petitions; 3) persistent demands; 4) demonstrations; 5) protests; 6) demonstration projects; 7) direct contact with legislatures or officials; or 8) additional activities mentioned in the section on self-reform of therapists which can be applied to other groups. Further kinds of activities can emanate from the creativity and ingenuity of the individuals who comprise the group.

As a final word, we cannot overemphasize the importance of energy in undertaking and sustaining social action. Indeed, at different stages of progress toward social change energy may be more important than clarity of objectives and strategies since such precision is very difficult to achieve in the social realm. At any given time it may be the energy which sustains the effort when goals and strategies are being re-evaluated. As the effort gains time, momentum, and experience as the result of the energy of the participants, more precise definitions and specific strategies will follow. This is not to say that individuals should strike out on a path toward social action without any direction, but that it is expended energy which makes possible the experiences that will give precision to the direction.

Change In Small Social Systems

Stress in individuals is seen as emanating from two possible sources: large social systems or small social systems. It is the latter of these two that will be the present topic for discussion. For the purposes of this discussion, small social systems are defined as those which have effects on relatively small numbers of people. Individuals, families, couples, and social and occupational peer groups are examples of small social systems. When a group or family is experiencing stress, disorganization, or other kind of recognized or unrecognized turmoil, it is usually an individual rather than all the members of the system who seeks out or is brought to counseling. This person, many times called the identified patient, serves as an outward manifestation of a problem that usually encompasses all the members of the system. When a patient is identified, the burden of responsibility is usually lifted from the remaining members. There is now someone to blame, someone to label as the "problem person." It is not the system or the interrelationships that are at fault but rather the fault rests with the identified patient. In families this identified patient is most often the child who is behaving in a socially deviant or delinquent manner. The parent may then bring a shoplifting son to counseling or therapy saying, "Fix him! Make him be good so he isn't a problem to our family." The Social Change Counselor, as has been stated many times previously, does not see individuals' problems as caused from within but rather as responses to external stress. Whenever possible the activist counselor works with the small social system in its entirety, not the identified patient or scapegoat. The first part of this discussion will present techniques for working with and changing small social systems when members of those systems agree to take part in counseling. The last part of the discussion will suggest some techniques that may be used when system members are uncooperative and will not take part in counseling.

The initial steps in working with members of a small social system do not differ significantly from working with individuals who are having problems with large social systems. The counselor gives support to those who feel the stress of the system and again shares feelings or actions which are similar to those of the clients. By offering a political/social analysis of the problem situation and teaching the clients how to make analyses in this way, the counselor helps the members of the system move toward the identification of the real issues which are the source of the problem. Most often these issues center around power, control, and dependency. All may encounter difficulty in trying to locate the issue behind such presenting problems as sexual difficulties, disagreement over child discipline, division of responsibilities, lack of consideration for others, or incompatible life styles. These problems are most often manifestations of such issues as disparate definitions of acceptable levels of dependency and differential values regarding amount and desirability of the use of control.

Once the members of the system are able to identify and are aware of the dependency and power struggles taking place, they are all faced with the three possible options presented in the previous section:

1. Remain in the problem situation, making no changes or adjustments, but with an awareness of the source of the problems.
2. Learn to live with (adjust to) the problem situation. The clients change their behavior or thoughts about the problem, but the situation or relationships remain unchanged.
3. Change the behaviors and relationships within the small social system that are causing the stress.

When all members of the system choose to exercise the third option, the techniques which follow can be employed. However, when they choose to exercise different options, the system becomes one in which there is less than total cooperation, and the techniques designed for an uncooperative system must be employed. Those techniques will be described at a later point.

When all are agreed that change of the system is needed, several steps follow. Awareness of weaknesses in the system and talking about problem relationships are good first steps but only action will change those systems and relationships. For this reason the members should discuss and offer suggestions for concrete ways to alter the situation. The counselor or therapist can offer additional suggestions and assist the members in implementing the actions they wish to take. Members could possibly negotiate a contract, sharing responsibilities, and agreeing to act in ways that will alter the power and dependency relationships. In this method, one or more individuals agree to change their ways of acting if others agree to change their actions. Another useful technique involves restricting the environment so that either the problem does not arise again, or, if it should arise, it will not be sustained. Moving to a larger house with more living space has helped many a family whose living conditions had made life intolerable for all involved. An additional technique for changing small social systems constitutes a realignment of the power or dependency structures. While implementing this technique, experiences in role reversal can provide valuable insights into and awareness of the feelings accompanying a role in the power structure that is the reverse of the one the individual presently occupies. When the controller and the controlled change places, or a dependency relationship is reversed, the effects of the structure, experiences and feelings of other system members, are more meaningful. A democratic realignment of power creates a more desirable living and working environment though initial reactions to such a change may be difficult. To make the transition an easier one, the counselor can assist the system members in practicing their new roles (via realistic role play, and/or commenting on their interactions during the interview) to see how former conflict situations will and can change as a result of these new roles. It can be expected that one or more individuals within a system might need additional support, practice, or experiences beyond what the group requires. Assertive training, structured experiences outside the actual system, and/or other devices can be constructed to give added strength and skills to an individual member. The counselor needs to be involved in this instruction or in referring the client to outside sources.

Assertive training in particular holds promise as a skill which is teachable and easily transferable. It provides an individual system member with experience and expertise which will aid him/her in reaching and maintaining a desired role, especially in dependency relationships.

As mentioned previously, working with a system in which one or more members are uncooperative or refuse to take part in the counseling and/or change process necessitates the use of different techniques. In such cases the counselor or therapist works with the person or persons who want to alter the system to make it less stressful and oppressive. Commonly men are found to be less willing to take part in counseling than women. Part of this unwillingness is perpetuated by the myth that men should be able to handle their own problems, whereas women are legitimate in seeking help because they are weak and at the mercy of their emotions. Further, men often recognize that they have disproportionate amounts of power and control in small social systems and therefore are unwilling to risk engaging in activities which might weaken their position.

The task of the counselor in cases where total cooperation cannot be enlisted centers on supporting and strengthening those willing to make changes in the system. When more than one individual accepts the need for change, the counselor can teach them how to be mutually supportive of each other's feelings and attempts to change. The counselor can also act as an advocate for children struggling under oppressive family structures by seeking change through legal, social, or other avenues. System members may issue ultimatums (which they must be prepared to carry out) to uncooperative members, demanding their participation in the change process. The text of the ultimatum usually requires that certain actions be taken, or the member working for change will leave that system. Because there are many alternative types of small social systems, leaving such an oppressive system is easier than finding alternatives when oppressed by a large social system. However, the authors advocate activity to change oppressive small social systems rather than leaving them, since other systems are also likely to create stressful environments. In addition, oppressive ideologies which are not confronted on a small scale tend to be carried over to large social systems and are maintained there, having an effect on an even greater number of people.

When an individual has enough strength to implement change in a system, other members (both cooperative and uncooperative) will react in one of three possible ways:

1. One or more members may welcome and reinforce the changes thereby increasing the likelihood of further change. In most cases this outcome is desirable because a smaller amount of trauma is created.
2. One or more members may respond so negatively that the change agent(s) has neither the emotional nor physical strength to maintain his/her change activities. Following such a development, the change agent(s) may fall back into previous patterns of dealing with the stressful environment, may try to learn to live with (adjust to) the situation, or may leave and seek out an alternative environment.
3. The activities of the change agent(s) may cause the system to become disorganized such that the resultant stress would cause one or more of the uncooperative members to either ask for individual assistance (from the counselor) or participate in the change process.

Both client(s) and counselor should be aware of these possible outcomes of implementing change in small social systems and be prepared for such consequences by assessing the risk involved.

Conclusion

As advised earlier, the techniques are admittedly sketchy both because practical applications of the theory of Social Change Counseling are still in the early stages of development and because the techniques must be altered and reworked to fit particular cases and specific problem systems. It is hoped that readers who agree with the philosophical tenets of the Social Change approach will expand upon the information and suggestions that have been presented here and will work toward the change of society's oppressive institutions and systems.

4

Theoretical Comparisons and Case Examples

This chapter is an attempt to give some of the flavor of Social Change Counseling through actual examples. Suffice it to say that the style of an activist counselor will tend to be informal. The counselor will usually relate to the client as a personal friend. This means less distance, a rejection of the rule that the therapist cannot talk about his/her own experiences when they are appropriate, perhaps less rigidity about when and where the encounter takes place, and flexible counseling time periods.

It is recognized that these variations might be initially disconcerting for the client. The counseling experience will probably be unlike any he/she has had before. This does, however, set the stage for the therapist to explain completely what can happen in therapy, how the therapist expects to function in that process, and what might be the possible consequences. This initial openness will lay the groundwork for a non-hierarchical relationship between client and counselor. This is perhaps one of the most difficult changes for an already practicing counselor to make. Constant vigilance and help from others via tapes of sessions, will be needed to combat this tendency to be in charge.

An inherent part of this counseling approach rests on the awareness of the counselor and his/her ability to translate that awareness into helping a client achieve a political perspective about a presenting problem. Therefore, the first step in our presentation of examples will be to cite well-known counseling references and examine and contrast the interpretations which are given to client behavior and verbalizations.

Theoretical Comparisons

Carl Rogers, in *On Becoming a Person* (1961), cites seven stages in the therapy process with representative client statements. In stage one, Rogers reports the client is unaware of his/her problems and has no desire for change. A statement such as "I think I'm practically healthy," might be made (p. 132). A Social Change approach might reaffirm that the person seems healthy to the therapist also. The belief that often when one feels the most healthy it seems as if he/she fits in least would be shared. Some statement about trying to live a healthy and happy life in a world that is certainly neither of those might be made. The therapist would share an example of feeling "healthy" and what it was like when he/she did not. The initial statement perhaps reflects some uncertainty which may be coming from others, telling the client that he/she is not healthy. An open question, asking if there is any evidence that he/she is not healthy, might be advanced when the client discusses situations concerning his/her environment which do not make sense. The therapist would attempt to find a political reason behind the circumstances, thereby confirming the reality of the person, that the situation really did happen the way he/she perceived it. Following this, the road to discovering why events happen in this culture would be undertaken.

In an additional excerpt, from stage three, Rogers hypothesizes that there is a loosening of expression but personal constructs remain rigid, for example: "I feel guilty for so much of my young life that I expect I felt I deserved to be punished most of the time anyway [p. 136]." Rogers comments that he sees this as a constructed experience and not a settled fact. Approaching the response differently, a society-oriented counselor might reflect that the great amount of guilt which is felt by our citizens as a whole is at least partially indicative of the pervasiveness of that socialization. Guilt has been systematically taught to nearly everyone by the legal code and by religious organizations and is used by those in authority as a way to maintain control and power. Guilt is a key to maintaining oppression because anyone who feels guilty will not outwardly express his/her anger and consequently will not be attempting to change the current power system. Finally, the therapist would share feelings of guilt which he/she feels or has felt and would mention how political awareness had helped, or was helping to alleviate some of those feelings.

Rogers' stage four is represented by feelings of being accepted by the therapist and new awareness of other feelings (including distrust and fear), for example: "I feel bound by something or other. It must be me! There's nothing else that seems to be doing it. I can't blame it on anything else. It makes me want to get mad and cry and run away!" This sort of revelation would be met very sympathetically by a counselor who is aware that the environment can sometimes be constricting, and that the pressures, because they are not tangible, are interpreted by the client to be a product of his/her own mind. Some sharing, to help the client learn that similar feelings had been felt by the counselor or others, would precede an attempt to find what is exerting the pressure. Throughout, the client would be reassured that it is not a personal deficit and perhaps not even uncommon to experience such tensions, but that one often feels that it is a personal fault because others do not seem to perceive stimuli in a similar manner. Finally, it can be explained that paranoid feelings are often a reflection of true reality and only the client is attuned to them.

Walter Kempler in *Gestalt Therapy Now* (1970) gives a sample initial interview with a family: husband, wife and two sons, ages 12 and 15. The interchanges are primarily between the woman and the therapist regarding problems they are having with one son, and the disagreement on discipline which exists between the parents. The husband is then provoked from a submissive position in which he states that he is sure his wife is doing as well as she can. The therapist responds, "You know as well as I that if you want her off your back, you just have to tell her to get the hell off your back and mean it," later adding, "If I'm wrong, be man enough to disagree with me, and don't wait to get outside of here to whimper to your wife . . ." After the husband expresses his anger at the therapist, the therapist asks him to direct it to any other family member. He responds to the challenge and tells his wife, "He's right. I take an awful lot of nonsense from you and I hate it. I don't intend to take any more. I'll settle with the kids my way. If you don't like it, that's too bad." The therapist tells the man, "I like you better when you are being the man I know you are." The therapist adds in the notes that "On the few subsequent visits, the father ushered his family in [pp. 157–159]."

In this encounter the therapist was operating from and reinforcing the belief and value that men should speak firmly and outright, and that they should take charge of their families in a seemingly dictatorial manner. An activist counselor would approach the family in a markedly different manner. He/she would meet with all the family and initially introduce his/her beliefs about families in an attempt to make the values explicit. The therapist would then ask each family member to explain how they perceived the problem, what change(s) might be helpful for them, and how those changes might be accomplished. The therapist would not maintain that fathers or mothers of adolescent offspring are rightly a controlling force. A move to democratic decisions would be encouraged. The therapist might suggest for the family members some reading material by David Cooper, or other contemporary analyzers of modern western families. Through the reading and discussion the therapist would encourage each family member to examine the influence the family was having on him/her: how individual or several members oppressed, victimized or controlled other members; the similarities between their family and others they know; and what values they had about families, their interaction, and their rules. This might be done totally within the context of the one family, or, after some initial progress is made and awareness achieved, the family as a whole might join a group of other families. An additional option would be for the parents and offspring to meet in separate groups with their own peers and then come together for family sessions.

Rational Emotive Therapy (RET) examples usually show that an extreme amount of permission is given to persons or families to feel and think the way they would like. The Social Change approach concurs with this aspect of RET. Additionally, much of RET is geared to self-help or at least a group approach which is consistent with a societal orientation. Unfortunately, however, because anger is believed to be a negative emotion, and therefore undesirable and expendable, social change can never occur from RET. The belief that others, or institutions, should be responsible for acts or consequences of their acts is countered by rational thinking. No one is ever to blame for the ways in which things work out. Therefore no one can be called to account for making changes. It is this aspect of RET with which the authors disagree.

Many behavioral techniques, particularly those oriented toward individuals instead of groups, seem highly appropriate to the authors. Teaching maintenance behaviors to a retarded child, controlling eating behaviors in an anorexic, encouraging information-seeking behavior for career development, and elimination of phobias all are highly valuable ways to encourage the freedom of persons. Many are not directly related to oppressive situations. However, others' uses of the principles of behavior modification are distinctly designed to maintain control and the status quo. The token economy as it is often used in juvenile homes, prisons, or mental hospitals encourages reduction of conflict, conformity, and behavior which will maintain the status quo. Inmates are truly taught "appropriate" social behavior. No one asks if that style of relating will be appropriate for the environments to which they will return or discusses the inherent problems in the middle-class style of relating. Mental hospital patients are usually rewarded for passive behavior which will not interfere with the hospital's operation. Unfortunately, these are not the behaviors which will be needed to return to the outside world.

Similarly, dating skills or social skills groups encourage people to engage in social interaction which is possibly beneficial to them. The opportunity is seldom seized to teach other-than-traditional sex-role behaviors.

The authors believe that the technology and principles of behavior modification are sufficiently refined that results can be predicted with near certainty. Therefore, it is time for serious thought to be given to the goals which clients are encouraged to pursue. Behavior modification proponents have often said that the technology is value-free. This is correct. At its moment of application, however, political and social issues are raised. They must not be considered value-free.

Following the basic format which was used in the preceding techniques chapter, this chapter will continue by presenting examples of self-reform, change in large social systems and change in small social systems.

Self-Reform Examples

This section will include two examples of efforts to change consciousness and awareness. The first example concerns a women's group consisting of counselors and others in various helping professions who wanted to gain awareness about the political nature of problems peculiar to women. The second example illustrates the learning which can be accrued from involvement in grass roots political organizing.

For the past two years an organization called Women's Exchange has existed in Lafayette, Indiana, which has had two primary objectives: first to provide a source of assistance to women in the geographic area, and second to offer support and consciousness-changing experiences for the members of Women's Exchange. The nature of assistance varied between individual contact with members of Women's Exchange, referral to women's groups, or referral to an agency or professional in the community who could be of help.

All members had an interest in women's issues but were in various stages of consciousness, political knowledge, and awareness of published material concerning women. All members, however, knew that they could learn and benefit from experience in analyzing problems from a political perspective. The group decided before any assistance could be given to others, self-help was needed. Therefore, the twelve members met weekly to do problem sharing. Different members in turn would volunteer to form a team of two primary listeners to work with another member who wanted to discuss an issue or problem that was troubling her. The two primary listeners then proceeded to listen, interact, and talk with the woman as if she were a woman who had called the organization. After an initial period of time, during which the three women achieved some initial rapport and understanding, any other member of the group who wanted to speak to the woman who had presented the problem was encouraged to join in the discussion.

The process between the three usually included initial listening so that the presenter felt understood (basic listening skills training preceded this stage), some disclosure by one or both of the listeners regarding similar feelings, and some initial conjecture about the reasons such situations developed. The goal was to achieve rapport, share experiences, and gain some political awareness.

Following the discussion which ensued, a feed-back session was held for the listeners. First, the presenter commented about how she felt, what particular statements or attitudes had been helpful, and suggestions she had about what would have been useful. Secondly, other members of the group, who had been observing the interaction, commented on the same criteria.

Over the course of several months, it was found that members gained insight into possible political analysis of situations and increased their comfort in discussing that with others. When the organization began receiving calls from women in the community, a team of two listeners met with the caller and followed approximately the same format. Case conferences were used at that time — often involving role playing of the caller — to facilitate the listener's ability to perceive the situation. In addition to the problem-sharing and case conferences the members of the organization experienced for themselves the starting of a women's group like the ones to which callers were referred. This included a discussion of goals, uses of power by individual members and the temporary leaders, the parallels of the group's power structure to other systems, and ways to change power lines.

These three self-help plans enabled those who were professional counselors to transfer insights about their relating style to their professional clients. Although this particular self-help plan was organized in conjunction with a new community organization, it could easily be adopted within any agency or group of counselors who would like to modify their counseling style in the direction of more awareness of political and social factors. Likewise, although this group focused on women's problems, which facilitated the use of problem-sharing, other topical groups such as families, students, sex, or employees would be easily identifiable for most counselors. For groups with which one does not identify: welfare recipients, blacks, gay, or lower-class, role-plays would have to be substituted for problem sharing. The authors recommend this experiential approach as a prime method of consciousness changing.

The second example refers to a colleague, Bob, who as a graduate student lived in a low-rent housing district. During the time he was living there, some of his neighbors began talking about tenant organizing. Although he intended to remain in the housing project for only a year until he finished school, he decided that exposure to the workings of political organizing and its problems would be a good educational experience. During this year of work with his neighbors he gained a perspective which was unlike his previous middle-class white orientation to city government and its officials. He found that the power structure in obvious and subtle ways lends support to the landlord, that logic and reason would not persuade heretofore "reasonable" persons to consider a new perspective. Primarily, however, Bob gained an appreciation of the plight of welfare mothers, and learned that the acts of other social classes, which might appear deviant from a middle-class perspective, have intelligibility and meaning when viewed from the vantage point of the persons involved.

It is the authors' opinion that political involvement at grass-roots levels will produce insights and learnings which cannot be achieved on the campus or in the therapy session. Because many do not find themselves in situations in which they will be identifying with different social, ethic, or religious groups, and because this learning does need to come through that identification, many may find this example of self-reform more difficult to structure for themselves. However, block organizing for needed lighting, neighborhood playground equipment, or to protest a re-zoning will closely approximate the experience we are suggesting. Therefore, be aware of issues in your own community or neighborhood about which, and for which, you would organize. Begin encouraging others to join you and soon you will be having a true educational experience.

Large Social System Examples

Our examples of change in large social systems are from the community, the public schools, and a state mental hospital. They illustrate the principles of Social Change Counseling clearly because each of the problems are seen as a result of an environment which needs changing, not an individual.

The first example comes from an elementary school and was related to us by a young friend, Patti. Patti was, at the time of this incident, a fifth-grade student in an elementary school which drew its population from a broad spectrum of socio-economic classes. The counselor was a graduate student who was employed half-time by the county school district to serve this elementary school of 1200 students.

Patti went to her counselor one day because the advent of spring had shown her that there was not much for girls to do during recess and the noon hour following lunch. She liked sports and games but there were not many that girls could play because the only equipment (kick balls, softball and bats) were specifically designated for the boys of each grade. Patti thought this unfair and wanted some adult counsel and consultation on the matter. Her counselor responded, we feel, in a highly appropriate manner and encouraged Patti and any of her friends who felt similarly to plan something to do to correct the situation. The following day Patti and three other classmates arrived at the counselor's office. They had decided they wanted to talk to the principal about it. As an alternative the counselor suggested they could make a tape in her office which could be given to the principal. The four girls organized their case, and in turn presented it for the recording. Following this session, Patti thought of some additional facts to support their position and wrote a letter to be attached to the cassette tape. The four fifth-graders met briefly with the principal and gave him their tape and letter. We are pleased to report that the principal responded quickly and appropriately. The number of balls, bats, and kickballs which belonged to the school was promptly doubled with half of them now bearing the identification tag for girls of each grade.

Patti and her friends are proud of their accomplishment. Through the counselor's encouragement they planned a course of action which would confront the power source (the principal) in a logical and appropriate manner, one that would allow him to respond from a non-defensive posture. These young women learned that social change is possible and that one must plan and carry through a strategy designed to initiate change. It is believed by the authors that students should be counseled and encouraged to initiate procedures which will change those aspects of their school situation which are undesirable.

Our second example concerns an adolescent ward of a state hospital. The ward was headed by a chief psychologist (who earned a master's degree in psychology *after* being in charge of the ward for ten years) and a social worker (also without experience or training). A large group of aides and technicians rounded out the staff. The latter group was made up of college graduates, although no degree was specified. The patients of the ward were predominantly poor and had been referred to the hospital by their parents or from the juvenile court system. They were not evaluated at the time of their arrival, nor were any treatment plans derived individually or collectively. Their problems were primarily social, not psychological. Most had been improperly socialized according to the norms of their parents or police and/or were acting in a delinquent manner.

The treatment program consisted of one ward meeting every morning for all 30 patients and the staff (excluding the head). This group was supposed to function on the peer-influence model and talk about how they had been relating to each other in order to improve their relationships. There seemed to be at least tacit recognition that the problems were social and not psychological but the system which was used was highly ineffective. The 30 patients were usually highly verbal and angry and used the time to explode at each other. The aides, who were untrained in any treatment orientation, usually tried to encourage them to act differently and/or bawled them out for past failures.

The aides and technicians, however, were not satisfied with the level of treatment which was being given and began to organize across the shifts. They organized their grievances which included the following: 1) the patients had no individual or collective goals, 2) decisions were made in a crisis and were not consistent with any overall philosophy, 3) the aides and technicians carried the primary "treatment" responsibilities, but were not allowed to have input into any decisions regarding the patients. They took these grievances to their director's supervisor (they were refused an appointment with the hospital superintendent), and to a congressman who served on the state committee for mental health facilities. They soon found that tenure was a higher drawing card than incompetence and nothing would be done by the authorities. The chief psychologist, hearing of the activities, withdrew completely from contact with the staff but continued in his position.

Fortunately for the organizing staff, personal misconduct on the part of the director was sufficient for removal and this person was as guilty of inappropriate behavior as incompetence. The staff, therefore, proceeded to document his personal indiscretions, because these alone would produce the change that was sorely needed. Within a few months, this documentation caused the removal of the director, and he was replaced with a person who was able to give the leadership and direction which was needed. She did intake evaluations, planned programs for each patient, organized a variety of small groups, and offered consultation to the aides who continued to have primary contact with the adolescents.

This case does not have the happy ending which would be preferred. It is apparent that poor job performance when one is at the top is seldom a sufficient cause for change. However, when change is badly desired, and desperately needed, other means can be derived. This illustrates the need for determination and continued effort when the first plan does not produce success.

Our third example of change in a large social system results from a program which is currently underway. Representatives from several agencies which directly or indirectly are responsible for serving the youth of a community decided a group of teenagers aged 12–14 could be formed who could learn group interaction, group processes, and eventually have an impact on changing their milieu. One dozen youths in this age range were chosen and invited to a training weekend. Those chosen are primarily youth who are not affiliated with school organizations or other identity groups. They are all from families of a low socio-economic class. Many of their older siblings have had trouble with school or law enforcement authorities. They have not had experience in belonging, processing, making decisions, or planning action in advance.

The adults who initiated the program are committed to allowing the participants to determine their course of action. However, it was decided that most of the youths lacked the skills for involvement in this sort of project. The training weekend endeavored to overcome some of those deficiencies, and provide some common experiences which might facilitate their unification as a group. The initial day of the weekend proved to be a test for all concerned. The youth were unaccustomed to making group decisions and being responsible for their own progress, and problems developed between the sponsors and the youths. Agendas were put aside and the conflicts were talked through. With the exception of two boys, they all achieved some degree of group cohesiveness. Those two will receive some individual consultation, primarily in communication skills, with encouragement to rejoin the group as soon as possible.

The long-term goal of this group is to provide a base for young people to confront existing systems to which they belong, in the hopes of initiating change. They also will choose various community service projects in which they have an interest. The group's focus, particularly during the formative months, will consist of social activities blended with group exercises to practice decision making, increase communication skills, relate to and confront authority, and constructively resolve conflict and differences of opinion.

Although the project has not been underway long enough to assess adequately the impact that will be had by this new coalition of youth, the community centers and their junior high will most certainly be among those who will be tested for their responsiveness to the needs of its constituents.

Small Social System Examples

The two examples which follow illustrate change in small social systems and deal with counseling contacts with individuals and their subsequent effects on a small system, specifically the individuals' families. Small systems also include contact with individuals or a group of individuals for change within a social peer group, or group of employees. The following two examples were shared with us by colleagues.

Carol is a 22-year-old woman of working-class status. Although she quit high school at sixteen, she has never been employed and continued to live at home with her parents and younger siblings. She was referred to Women's Exchange by her physician following some gynecological surgery. She is an attractive woman and was neatly dressed at the time of her first appointment. Carol initially acted very hysterical, crying, fidgeting, and exclaiming repeatedly, "I don't want to go to the psychiatrist." Carol began the interview by asking the Women's Exchange listener questions about her such as "What's your job?" "What do you do?" After a series of questions which the listener answered completely and honestly, Carol appeared more comfortable and began talking about her situation.

Carol was referred because she does not trust other people and because her family "thinks she is crazy." They think she is crazy because she believes that men use her, that women should earn as much as men, that some people seem to get many bad breaks while others do not, and that people are dishonest and two-faced because they talk about other people behind their backs. She was presently particularly afraid of men. She had been engaged once since leaving high school but her fiancé left town unexpectedly. Her life was stymied by her fright. She could not apply for a job, did not have a driver's license and had few social contacts. Her family's expectations that she begin entering the world, and their labeling of her thoughts and beliefs (and therefore her) as crazy produced mixed messages for her.

Carol's responses in the initial and the five subsequent contacts were that it is "so good to know I'm not crazy." The last three sessions were devoted to making plans for Carol's reentry into the world. She felt strong enough to apply for a job and followed that by moving from the home of her parents. She was making initial social contacts with members of both sexes. She joined a women's group with which she has had contact for several months and presently is working with the volunteers who are opening a local women's center. Although Carol's awareness has not made significant changes in her larger world, it produced drastic and rapid alterations in the way she relates to her family and younger siblings.

It would be easy perhaps to ascribe this rapid and dramatic change to some outside force, to chance or at least to something besides six hours of sharing with other women. However, similar results have been found with other referrants to Women's Exchange and with women who are seen in professional clinics when they are related to in a sharing and political analysis style. Permission for feelings and an explanation for the situations in which women find themselves, seem to be a strong catalyst for change. The change is subsequently felt by the small social system.

Our second example for influencing change in a small social system is Ken, an 18-year-old middle-class, high school graduate. Ken's father is a very religious man and a career officer in the armed services. Ken's mother is a quiet woman who is a homemaker who believes her husband should have the primary disciplinary responsibilities. Her contact with Ken and his younger two brothers and sister has been somewhat superficial. Ken made contact with a community agency at a time when he was very depressed and suicidal. Since his graduation from high school several months earlier, he had continued to live at home, walked the streets, and argued with his father. His father had on occasion become irritated and locked Ken out of the house. Their primary area of disagreement was Ken's lack of goal direction; he had strongly conflicted with his father on this topic. Ken did not believe that a person had to be goal-directed, and he had not found any occupational area which was interesting to him.

Ken reported a history of nervousness throughout high school which included ulcers and occasional medication. This nervousness was strongly related to the conflict with his father, and it was manifested when Ken was confronted with tasks which his father had defined as very important, e.g., physics exams, standardized tests, and math homework. Ken expressed little interest, and only moderate aptitude for science and math. His favorite subjects had been literature and drama but his father had prohibited much emphasis in those areas.

Another area of marked difference between Ken and his family concerned religion. Although he had always been involved in church activities as an adolescent, he did not feel he had ever chosen that path, or ever even made a conscious choice. It was the expected thing in this family. Ken's problems with his father had caused dissension among other family members as they were drawn in on one side or the other.

Ken's initial contact with the counselor provided some conflict for her. He was obviously depressed enough that suicide was a real possibility. He had just returned from boot camp. He had tried to enlist in one of the armed services but had been discharged for "nerves" before he completed basic training. Ken interpreted this as his final defeat. He had failed in his own life style and had decided to try to follow his father's advice. That too had been futile and had ended in failure. The counselor's reaction was one of support. Believing that Ken did not have anyone else who was currently supporting him, she took him to the local food co-op where he could meet some people who would share Ken's political and social values. She decided that activity would be preferable to institutionalization. She made an appointment to see him the following day after mapping out a full schedule of activities and plans for him to do that evening.

Ken met with the counselor for twelve more sessions. During this time he explored what values he did want to choose for his own life. Many of these conflicted with those which he had been taught in his family. His counselor shared her own problems and present and past feelings about resolving the style of life, values, and beliefs which she wanted to hold. His counselor made extensive use of bibliotherapy. Modern theology and materials which presented political and social issues with a non-traditional analysis were extensively used by Ken as he struggled to discern his own opinions. During this time his conflict with his father continued. Ken was, however, able to separate himself from it so that he could decide he would never meet his father's expectations. He obtained a laborer's job which gave him the financial independence to live by himself. Ken continued reading avidly and reveled in the support which it gave him.

Ken perceived that his younger siblings would also face many of the problems which he had encountered. Their home life had never allowed any of them to make decisions or express opinions which were contrary to their father's authoritarian and religious orientation. The father, however, forbade any of the other siblings to see the counselor following Ken's move from the home. Ken, therefore, decided that he must help them himself, which he has been attempting. He is maintaining contact with his brothers and sister and, to a limited extent, with his mother.

A follow-up several months later revealed Ken had decided he would like to pursue his education so that he could become a social worker. The counselor encouraged him to continue exploration into many occupations as she felt he may have chosen that field because he was familiar with it via their contact.

Ken's clarification of values is perhaps more striking because of the vast divergence between him and his father. However, the choosing of one's beliefs about the world is a developmental step for all persons. Many, however, choose those which they were taught as children by default because the encouragement to examine other values is never given. They are unaware of alternatives, and/or the process of change is unknown to them. In this realm the political role of the counselor is obvious. His/her own values must be made explicit. Referrals to others with different points of view must be a possibility for any counselor.

Through his values clarification, Ken achieved a personal stability which he had not known. He also was able, through his own increased awareness and assuredness, to share that with his siblings in an effort to alleviate some of their stress.

5

Implications for Counselor Education

It is probably apparent to the reader that the orientation which we are advocating is one which is currently outside the mainstream of counselor education. Although recent journals have carried many examples of different counselors and student personnel workers advocating such approaches in one form or another, no translation has yet been made to the changes that are needed in the education of the practitioner.

The authors believe a program which would teach the skills for involvement as a Social Change Counselor, a change agent or a radical therapist could be designed. The initial steps, however, are crucial. Addition of a techniques of social change course will not suffice, nor will a practicum, social change theory course, or any other single or group of courses. We firmly advocate a restructuring of the philosophy of the department as a critical first step. This new philosophy must include several basic components. First, the professorial staff must agree that problems which look like individual malfunctions can often be traced to the result of a social system or cultural system which needs to be modified or changed. Second, this belief needs to be integrated into all existing courses so that this method of thinking becomes natural and spontaneous to professors and trainees as one alternative when considering a problem. Third, because course work alone will not provide the understandings and style of relating which are crucial to this approach, the program must contain a heavy component of experiential opportunities and requirements. Last, and of utmost importance, is the involvement of the faculty in the process of change. The value of role-models and experience by the faculty in the material to be presented cannot be underestimated. It is this final factor which will provide the impetus and the strength to the program. It must not be excluded or other changes will be half-hearted, inconsistent and elitist. It is here that change can be instigated by a single faculty member through discussions with colleagues highlighting how such an approach might fit into existing courses. As the ideas gain support it will be possible to consider making changes in the academic and experiential requirements.

There are additional changes which need to be considered which deal directly with the faculty. It is as crucial that the hierarchies be eliminated between teacher and learner as it is that they be eliminated between counselor and client. When a co-learner atmosphere can be established, which must be participated in by the faculty, the freedom to grow and change as individuals will be possible. Additionally, the faculty must begin to take political stands on issues which are crucial to the profession. This needs to be done within the professional organization on local, state, and national levels. The naive notion that counseling is apolitical must be squelched at every level from the counselor-client interaction to lobbying with legislatures and negotiating with school boards. Only by taking firm stands and proceeding with the necessary activist activities will funding and legislative changes be possible. The faculty member must also model a respecting attitude towards others who are in the helping professions, particularly those who are traditionally seen as lower on the hierarchy, such as nonprofessionals or social workers. Hierarchies between people who are striving toward mutual goals are a waste of energy and talent.

Those who are accepted as trainees in a counselor education program constitute a large variable of the output of that program. As long as grades, test scores, and previous campus involvement in legitimate organizations are the requirements for admission, those admitted will be the successes of the educational systems. They will be white and middle class. They will be less prone to confronting any educational system, for they achieved and were successful in it. A young activist who is committed to social change has likely not been involved in earning good grades, belonging to student government, or playing athletics. He/she will have spent time working in the community while reading and developing a philosophy which is not supported in the culture. These students must be encouraged to join the ranks of our profession.

Another large component of many graduate programs are teachers who earn their counseling courses during the summer or a year's sabbatical, or homemakers who have taught previously and are now planning to return to work. This group is such a large part of graduate programs because of the laws regarding counselor certification as they presently exist. Powerful teacher lobbying groups support laws which require teaching experience before counseling can be practiced. This enables a "logical" progression for teachers who want to continue their education. It also provides teachers with a good deal of influence over those who will become counselors. Counselors are certain to be sympathetic to teachers if they have been teachers for several years. These persons are also likely to support the status quo; their age, their experience, their conditioning, are going to render them less likely to consider change.

We are not advocating that college stars or ex-teachers be excluded from counselor education. That would be pure self-destruction as they constitute the majority of applicants. However, the ramifications of their exclusive selection must be considered. Additionally (perhaps initially), changes in state requirements specifying teacher experience and/or preparation must be initiated. A concerted effort which will involve considerable time and energy must be made; the price will not be too high. If the type of applicant is to change, the laws must be modified accordingly.

It is expected that programs will vary from institution to institution depending upon the chosen focus — public school counseling, student personnel, vocational rehabilitation, or community mental health — and the levels of training which they provide — master's, doctorate, or both. Additionally, the geographic location of a particular university will facilitate or hamper particular types of field placements which will be available. This latter variable may, in fact, largely determine what focus and level of training is appropriate for a given institution to undertake. This chapter will therefore identify possible courses and experiences which would be useful in a master's program; the concentration will vary and depend upon the focus which has been chosen by a department.

These recommendations are based on two suppositions. First, the extent of growth, experience, and learning which are incorporated in the training of a counselor requires two academic years.

Second, full-time study is heavily preferred over part-time or sporadic study in order to maximize the student's involvement and commitment. Some departments may find these two premises unacceptable or impossible. Depending on the extent to which they are compromised, the growth of the students and the potential for their involvement will be endangered.

The material and opportunities which the writers believe need to be included in a master's program will be divided into academic or classroom work, and experiential programs. Many of the classroom and experiential projects will need to be concurrent or consecutive but will be described separately at this point for clarity.

Academic courses which integrate theories of individual counseling with the theories and perspectives of social change would provide students with an opportunity to mesh these two sometimes conflicting viewpoints. A course in the political and sociological aspects of change, stressing theories of change, and techniques which have been used by others in large (nations) and small (families) systems would be advantageous. An analysis of the effect of power during change would be essential. Additionally, a course in deviance emphasizing the viewpoints of Szasz, Becker and Scheff would provide trainees with a new conception of those who differ from the norm. At some point early in the training, a discussion of the future of counseling and its impact on the culture must be included. This might be covered in a theories course, an orientation course, and/or the techniques and practicum courses.

Because of the power and effect of families and groups, both these small systems need individual study. This is to say that theories of their interactions and techniques of intervention must be included in the curriculum.

The research and statistics courses might well include a discussion of the uses of research in maintaining present oppressive conditions by supporting those in power and looking for alleged psychological deficits of those who are different.

The experiential component of the program contains essentially two thrusts: activities which will assist the trainee through individual growth and learning, and practice in the role of a counselor. In the first, each trainee needs involvement in a group which can provide a place to receive feedback about interpersonal functioning and clarify and explore his/her values. These need to include advanced graduate students and faculty so that a broader perspective is available. Microcounseling experiences in a lab setting, counseling, consulting, and initiating change would complement the theories course. In order for a trainee to gain information about the perspectives of clients, he/she should be encouraged to seek counseling from a department member or an outside source. In order to assimilate information about the organizational structure of an agency or a school counseling office, trainees could begin working in these settings doing non professional or ancillary tasks. They will learn about the work setting and have contact with professional counselors who will provide a host of learning experiences.

Placements or practicum experiences need to be individualized to meet the needs which are anticipated for the trainee's intended work situation, and also to broaden the perspective which he/she presently has. Cultural and socio-economic chauvinism is more likely to occur when the trainee has had little or no exposure to different types and groups of people. This possibility must be intentionally thwarted.

Following the microcounseling experience, the trainee will be prepared for the practicum experiences in individual, family, and group modes. Although the skills of individual counseling will be helpful in the latter two, supervised exposure in these domains is necessary as essential differences do exist. To highlight one or more of the courses which deals with change, an individual or group project could be included which would research a system, locate the true power sources, identify possible methods of intervention into that system, plan a strategy, and eventually implement at least one phase or aspect of the plan. This setting could be within a practicum, a work setting, a community center, neighborhood, or any other location with which the student had familiarity.

During the final semester every student would be encouraged to participate in a field experience in which he/she could function as a co-professional with the personnel employed there. The goal of this experience is not, however, to see if the trainee can "fit in," but rather to provide an additional setting in which the student can view professional counseling and analyze those aspects which are oppressive to the clientele. Hopefully the student will offer suggestions regarding changes which could be initiated by the counselors or the agency as a whole.

Because much of what is to be accomplished during the two years of training is growth, that is, growth in awareness, growth in understanding, and growth in skills, the writers advocate a criterion-based program and an end to traditional grading. The variables which are being considered are beyond ratings of good, better, or best. Additionally, grading systems engender and reinforce competition between peers. Since cooperation is a style which will serve the trainees as professionals, it needs to be modeled and reinforced during training. The completion of change projects will demonstrate mastery of change techniques; presentation of a successfully completed counseling case(s) will demonstrate skill in individual (or group or family) practicum; completion of a research project or a paper critiquing a particular series of research articles will adequately demonstrate research and statistical competency. A competency-based program will enable increased individualization within the program that is not possible when students are locked into semesters and grading. Although the amount of possible individualization will vary according to the size of the program, the number of faculty, and other available resources, freedom from grading will give increased flexibility and provide much needed accountability.

The modifications and changes which have been suggested are ones which will require much thought, work, and energy for any counselor education program to implement. However, therein lies the only hope for a change in the current state of counseling. We have not meant to imply that all counseling which is practiced is oppressive and counterproductive. However, much of what is done in the name of counseling is encouraging maintenance of the status quo. Often clients are encouraged to adjust to their environment. Those environments need confronting. Counselors must have the skills, awareness, and strength to wage those battles. Counselor training must meet this challenge; counselor educators must lead the way if change in programs is to occur and if trainees are to be prepared for their roles as change agents.

BIBLIOGRAPHY

Agel, J. (Ed.) *The radical therapist.* New York: Ballantine Books, 1971.

Agel, J. (Ed.) *Rough times.* New York: Ballantine Books, 1973.

Becker, H. S. *Outsiders.* New York: McMillan Co., 1963.

Bennis, W. G., Benne, K. D., Chin, R. (Eds.) *The planning of change* (2nd ed.). New York: Holt, Rinehart and Winston, 1969.

Boyers, R. (Ed.) *R. D. Laing and anti-psychiatry.* New York: Harper and Row, 1971.

Brown, P. (Ed.) *Radical psychology.* New York: Harper and Row, 1973.

Cooper, D. Being born into a family, in Brown, P. (Ed.), *Radical psychology.* New York: Harper and Row, 1973, pp. 156–174.

Eysenck, H. J. The effects of psychotherapy: an evaluation. *J. Consulting Psychology, 16,* 5, 319–324.

Fagan, J., & Shepherd, I. L. *Gestalt therapy now.* New York: Harper and Row, 1970.

Fanon, F. *The wretched of the earth.* New York: Grove Press, 1968.

Friedman, J. *Retracking America.* Garden City, New York: Doubleday, 1973.

Fromm, E. *The sane society,* New York: Holt, Rinehart and Winston, 1955.

Glenn, M., & Kunnes, R. *Repression or revolution?* New York: Harper and Row, 1973.

Halleck, S. L. *The politics of therapy.* New York: Harper and Row, 1971.

Honigman, J. J. *Personality in culture.* New York: Harper & Row, 1967.

Kempler, W. Experiential psychotherapy with families, in Fagan, J. and Shepherd, I. L. (Eds.), *Gestalt therapy now.* New York: Harper and Row, 1970, pp. 150–161.

Kittrie, N. N. *The right to be different.* Baltimore: Penguin Books, 1973.

Laing, R. D. *The divided self.* New York: Random House, 1960.

Laing, R. D. *The politics of experience.* New York: Ballantine Books, 1967.

Laing, R. D. *The politics of the family.* New York: Random House, 1972.

Laing, R. D., & Esterson, A. *Sanity, madness and the family.* Service Association, Baltimore: Penguin Books, 1970.

Manser, E. (Ed.) *Family advocacy.* New York: Family Service Association of America, 1973.

McKeon, R. (Ed.) *The basic works of Aristotle.* New York: Random House, 1941.

Merton, R. K. *Social theory and social structure.* (2nd ed.) The Free Press of Glencoe, 1957.

Millett, K. *Sexual politics.* New York: Avon Books, 1969.

Radical therapist, 1971, *1* (1); 1974, *4*, (2).

Redlich, F. C., & Freedman, D. X. *The theory and practice of psychiatry.* New York: Basic Books, 1969.

Reich, C. A. *The greening of America.* New York: Random House, 1970.

Rogers, C. R. *On becoming a person.* Boston: Houghton Mifflin Company, 1961.

Ruitenbeck, H. M. *Going crazy.* New York: Bantam Books, 1972.

Scheff, T. J. *Being mentally ill: a sociological theory.* Chicago: Aldine Publishing Co., 1966.

Steiner, C. Radical psychiatry manifesto, in Agel, J. (Ed.) *The radical therapist.* New York: Ballantine Books, 1971, pp. 280–283.

Szasz, T. S. *Ideology and insanity.* Garden City, New York: Doubleday and Company, 1970.

Toffler, A. *Future shock.* New York: Random House, 1970.

INDEX

ABCDEFGHIJ-M-8210/798765